False

Adequacy

By
Dr. Mark D. Michael

Harrison House
Tulsa, OK

19 18 17 16   10 9 8 7 6 5 4 3 2 1

False Adequacy: Finding God at the End of You

ISBN:978-168031-090-0

Copyright © by Dr. Mark D. Michael

Published by Harrison House Publishers

Tulsa, Oklahoma 74145

www.harrisonhouse.com

Table of Contents

Chapter 1

Are You Adequate?

In July of 2011, I had an experience that powerfully impacted my life. It wasn't something dramatic like someone close to me dying or that I was suffering from a major sickness. What happened to me was actually quite simple and ordinary—my car broke down. Nothing to get all bent out of shape about, I suppose, but for the first time in my life, I was without a car. This meant the loss of my independence and control. I felt so powerless! Did I also mention the fact that I didn't have the finances to fix it and was single and living alone at the time?

In the wake of my new reality, I had to employ a new means of transportation—walking. Luckily, I did not live very far from the local convenience and grocery stores. Yet, as an educated man and a minister of the gospel, not having my own car and having to resort to walking everywhere was beyond humiliating. I have always considered myself to be a humble person. As a matter of fact, if you would have asked someone who had known me for years if I was a proud man, they probably would have said, "No, in fact, he is a very humble guy." However, as I spent time praying and seeking God, He began to show me otherwise.

As I was walking to the store one day, I took the opportunity to witness to a certain man who lived on the streets. In my discourse, I told him that Jesus loves him and I encouraged him to give his life to the Lord. Using a line I had heard in my own life, I said, "You can live your life according to God's will, or you can live your life according to your own will." The man just looked at me kind of funny and replied, "I think I will live my life according to my own will."

Sadly, I realized that the only difference between me and this man was that until that moment, I did not realize that I had been following my own plans for my life. I had no idea that God's plan for my life could be so totally different from mine. It was during this time that the Holy Spirit spoke to me and said, "What you have been dealing with is called *false adequacy.*" I had never heard that phrase before, but somehow I understood what He was saying.

We all have an internal need to prove that we are adequate; that we are just as good as, or perhaps even better, than others. The word "adequate" means sufficient to fill a need or meet a requirement. The world views adequacy as a good thing, but that is not necessarily true in all instances. For example, in our school system we are taught that we can do anything we put our mind to. While this might be a good admonition, it creates in us an ambition to prove our worth; to show others that we measure up, and to prove to ourselves and others that we are capable.

This mindset can even effect how we hear the gospel. The core of the gospel is faith in the finished work of Jesus Christ on the Cross. Each time the gospel is presented, the listener has an important decision to make: *Am I adequate without God in my life or do I need this Jesus who is being preached to me?* If the battle within to prove adequacy is strong, they will reject the gospel of Jesus Christ in an effort to show God and others how "good" they are.

False adequacy begins with the erroneous idea that all we need from God is a ticket to heaven when we die, but down here on earth we can do for ourselves. It is the condition of living one's life independent from God, and it can be manifested in any area of our lives where we feel we can function without the direction and assistance of God.

Based on this definition, it's easy to see that the unsaved are not the only ones expressing false adequacy. Many born-again believers express false adequacy when they live their lives at a religious distance from God, embracing their humanity as adequate. In its simplest form, false adequacy is self-confidence. Most of us have been taught that having self-confidence is a good thing. In fact, many people are proud of their self-confidence, yet it is the way of the flesh and the way of the world. In the Kingdom of God, our confidence is in the Lord.

Not that we are sufficient of ourselves to think any thing as of ourselves, but our sufficiency is of God.

2 Corinthians 3:5

Notice that Paul, the writer of 2 Corinthians, did not seek to build his life on self-confidence. He understood that his adequacy came from God. False adequacy creates in us a selfish desire to prove that we are naturally or spiritually capable. Therefore, whether it is the desire to show others that we are smarter than they are, or the effort to preach without giving time to prayer, both denote false adequacy. False adequacy is relying on ourselves—our strength, our intellect, our wisdom, our influence, and our abilities—rather than on God.

Those who have false adequacy frustrate the grace of God by constantly applying their own human efforts in order to achieve the will of God. In their pride, they insist on relying on themselves. Yet, without complete reliance upon God, all of our feeble efforts in life and ministry are futile.

False adequacy influences what car we buy, where we choose to live, even whom we choose to marry. When we have false adequacy, we resist knowing what the will of God is for our lives because we are afraid it may contradict our own plans. When we offer up prayers, our prayers are for God's support in achieving our own plans, not for His will and direction. There is a big difference between humbly pursuing God's will for our lives and prayerfully pursuing our own will.

Exceptionality

Then said Elijah unto the people, I, even I only, remain a prophet of the LORD; but Baal's prophets are four hundred and fifty men.

1 Kings 18:22

False adequacy is predicated upon the pride of exceptionality. We all have an inner desire to be special and, in truth, we are all special to our heavenly Father. However, those who deal with false adequacy live to show others how exceptional or special they are. In the above scripture, Elijah decried, *"I am the only one still serving God!"* He could have said, "I am just one of many people serving the Lord," but instead, he focused on his own offering and service to God as if it made him the exceptional one.

False adequacy is born in our heart when we are impressed with some gift, ability, or aspect of ourselves. Individuals with false adequacy display in some way or another, a "Messiah Complex" or a "Chosen One Complex." They think things like: *I am the smartest guy in this company; Our church is the only one that is really serving God; If people would listen to me, their lives would be better; I only listen to my pastor because I know he teaches the truth; I don't know too many people who are as anointed as I am.* These kinds of thoughts generate a sense of exceptionality.

Have you ever wondered why people blindly join a cult and end up committing suicide at the behest of some deranged leader? Cults appeal to a person's desire to be "special." When a person joins a cult, it is usually because they have been deluded into believing that as a member of the cult, they are now a part of something exceptional. They have been led to believe that the rest of the world is in ignorance and cult members are the only ones who are truly "enlightened." They will give all they have to the control of the cult leader in exchange for the notion that they are exceptional.

Christians are not exempt from the struggle with false adequacy. Many Christians wrestle with this same idea that they are special. In order for God to break the false adequacy off of our lives, He has to first convince us that we are not special in and of ourselves, but He is special. This is not to say that we are not special in Christ, because we are. However, we have not been sent to earth to prove to the world that we are special. God sent us here so that we can show the world how special Jesus is.

The Search for Significance

We all strive to find significance in life; in fact, the search for significance is often much stronger than we realize. Today, people are both consciously and subconsciously seeking to prove their importance, sometimes by diminishing the importance of others.

And James and John, the sons of Zebedee, come unto him, saying, Master, we would that thou shouldest do for us whatsoever we shall desire. And he said unto them, What would ye that I should do for you? They said unto him, Grant unto us that we may sit, one on thy right hand, and the other on thy left hand, in thy glory.

Mark 10:35-37

James and John approached Jesus and made the request that they be allowed to sit on His right and left sides when He comes into His Kingdom. This was a presumptuous preemptive move, to say the least. These two disciples were seeking to place themselves in positions of significance above the other disciples. Sadly, this is still the case with many believers today. They seek to be prominent in some aspect of life. They are searching for significance.

Every person has within him a desire to be significant. To be significant is to matter in life and to have the respect, admiration, and honor of others. On a subconscious level, we are all striving for significance—whether we are running for a political office or feigning sickness for attention. The search for significance is often expressed in superlatives as we strive to be the smartest, most influential, most affluent, most attractive, funniest or strongest.

What makes you feel significant? Your clothing? Your car? Your skills? While we are searching to make our mark on the world, we may measure our progress by gauging our adequacy. *Do I have what it takes? Am I as good as others? Am I the greatest? Do I stand out above others?*

The greater our pride, the greater our search for significance will be. When we come under the lordship of Jesus, we surrender our search for significance and adopt a life dedicated to making Jesus significant. He is our example. He came to earth, not to do His own will, but to do the will of the Father. Jesus came into the world to save us and to glorify His Father. Glorifying Himself was not one of His goals.

> *Then said I, Lo, I come: in the volume of the book it is written of me, I delight to do thy will, O my God.*
>
> Psalm 40:7-8

I have glorified thee on the earth: I have finished the work which thou gavest me to do.

John 17:4

Just as Jesus came to earth to do the will of the Father and to glorify the Father, even so are we to walk in His footsteps. Our work is that of glorifying Jesus and doing His will. This is a great struggle for some modern-day believers. Today, we have believers who claim they love Jesus, yet they promote themselves. Though Jesus was humble, many desire to be Christians without being humble. They believe that God's desire is to save them, yet they refuse to believe that He also wants to be glorified in their lives.

Without Jesus in our lives, we can have no true significance. Many believers have embraced this world's affirmations of significance, believing they are important because they have a title or their name is on a desk or a billboard. However, God never intended for believers to look to these worldly forms of significance. Our significance comes from God and it is false adequacy to believe that it can be derived from anything else. God has made us significant in Christ!

Impressed with "Self"

False adequacy is distorted self-perception that begins with the belief that we are special, and then extends into a conscious or subconscious life of being impressed with ourselves. False adequacy causes us to overestimate our worth, to place value on ourselves that is inconsistent with the value that other people place on us.

For I say, through the grace given unto me, to every man that is among you, not to think of himself more highly than he ought to think; but to think soberly, according as God hath dealt to every man the measure of faith.

Romans 12:3

When we have false adequacy, we believe that we have what it takes in life. We may never formally say that we are impressed with ourselves, but if we live our lives without the input of God, that's basically what we are saying. When we are impressed with ourselves, we inherently believe that we are great. Therefore, we sit around waiting for God to show the world how great we are.

There is a very thin line between self-esteem and being impressed with oneself. While having self-esteem is a good thing, being impressed with oneself is not. Since being impressed with ourselves happens on a subconscious level, most of us are not even aware of it. It usually takes a highly embarrassing moment for a person to come to terms with his subconscious thoughts of greatness. Take, for instance, the person who believes he belongs in New York City on a Broadway stage when, in actuality, he is only an average performer on his own small town stage. A few auditions followed by crushing rejections will bring the falsity of his subconscious thoughts of greatness to light.

We all tend to be easily impressed with our gifts, talents, intellect, social skills, athleticism or abilities. Because of this, it is important that we not become our own standard in life. For example, if my singing in the shower is my standard for a great singing voice, I could be overly impressed with my ability to sing. Yet, when others hear me sing, they might not be as impressed with my singing as I am.

If I honor myself, my honor is nothing: it is my Father that honoreth me.

John 8:54

Jesus resisted the temptation to be impressed with Himself. He embraced honor from God. Since false adequacy is based on the belief that we are great, being honored by others is seen as evidence of this greatness. If honor is not received from others, we are only great in our own eyes. Therefore, we hold honor as an idol and want people to see and admire us, even if it means they fail to see and admire Jesus. The root of this is pride.

People who are impressed with themselves are often status seekers. Status seeking is the lust for promotion, both within the church and in corporate America. Promotion is the evidence and affirmation of adequacy. Therefore, those who are smitten by false adequacy are always seeking promotion or waiting on God for promotion. They cannot tolerate living an ordinary life with an ordinary job or an ordinary assignment because they are bent on the idea of being exceptional. They spend an inordinate amount of energy trying to associate themselves with success. They will not accept a supporting role because they are convinced that they should be the center of the show.

People who are impressed with themselves feel like they deserve a place of prominence or honor, regardless of merit. False adequacy minimizes the contributions of other people in a vain effort to take credit for any accomplishment. In other words, our goal becomes showing others how great we are because we are determined to receive recognition. Promotion that comes from God follows true humility and a realization that there is nothing special about us. There is only something special about the One who resides within us—Jesus! Paul, the Apostle, put it this way:

> *For I know that in me (that is, in my flesh) dwelleth no good thing.*
> Romans 7:18

Our gifts, talents, abilities, intellect, wisdom, looks, etc. are all endowments from God. When we humble ourselves and give the glory to God, He can promote us.

Dependency on God

False adequacy is a belief that we can go about the tasks of our lives without complete dependency and reliance upon God. We all have a certain degree of reliance upon God which can be evidenced by our church attendance or our religious practices. Yet many who attend church each week are totally oblivious to what it means to be dependent on the Father. Many saints who speak of God have not yielded to Him yet. One of the greatest tragedies of our day is the fact that we seek to do the work of God without the power of God!

Many people who have false adequacy are not aware of their condition. They simply live their lives pursuing their dreams and goals. Many are frustrated and tired by virtue of a life lived in their own strength. Then they become angry with God when their plans for greatness are not realized.

False adequacy is the desire to be blessed by God without having a relationship with Him. Often, we look at people who are blessed financially and we erroneously assume that the reason they are well off is because they are adequate. Our goal then becomes to prove that we are just as adequate, and we abandon the purpose of the Father in a vain effort to measure up to others in this life.

Many believers have become callous to the will of God because they are seeking a house, a spouse, two kids and a dog. The American dream becomes their new idol and the things of God must be put on the back burner until that goal is met. False adequacy is the arrogant disposition that says, "If I can figure out and work my way into success in life, I will be happy; but if I must submit to God and ask Him to bless me, I decline."

We all have a certain design for how we would like to see our lives unfold. Those who deal with false adequacy cling to this vision for their lives even in the face of utter failure. Their prayer may as well be, "Not as God wills, but as I will." We want the world to be what we dreamed it up to be. Consequently, we resist some aspects of the will of God if they don't align with our vision for our life. Our goal is to prove that we are the captain of our own ship and the master of our own world.

Humanism

Humanism is another form of false adequacy. God does not see men as great, but rather as depraved and in need of His salvation and strength. False adequacy does not acknowledge any lack, but prompts us to be something that we are not and do things that we are not gifted to do. When we have false adequacy, we have trouble saying, "I don't know" or "I am not good at that." We always feel compelled to prove that we can do anything and to show others that we are just as good as anyone else. To admit weakness would be to accept our limitations, and we are too proud for that!

False adequacy drives us to look financially endowed, when in fact, we are poor and impoverished. False adequacy causes us to suffer in silence because we are too proud to tell others what we need. False adequacy convinces us that it is disgraceful not to have all the answers. The pride that accompanies false adequacy makes us refuse instruction, thinking it is below us to be taught by someone else. When backed against a wall when we absolutely have to be taught, those of us who cling to false adequacy minimize the teaching experience by saying things like, "I understand it now; you don't have to show me anymore," or "I've got it from here." We are determined to prove that we are the ones who "know," and everyone else needs to learn from us.

False adequacy breeds a pride that refuses to receive instruction and is highly opinionated about everything. It may mean that we spend endlessly to win the lottery because our pride will not allow us to submit to God's financial instructions. For many believers, winning the lottery means living their life their way, without consulting or pleasing God.

False adequacy breeds rebellion. Those who have false adequacy hold contempt for any rules imposed on their lives. For example, the man who has been married three times and on the occasion of his fourth marriage, refuses marriage counseling on the presumption that he has marriage all figured out—he is a perfect example of false adequacy.

The prisons today are full of men and women who deal with false adequacy. They rebel against the rules of society and God because they insist that life should be the way they want it to be. There is a direct correlation between dependency on God and humility. The level of our reliance upon God is a big indicator of how humble we are and whether or not we are under the influence of false adequacy. Anytime we are not fully reliant upon God, we are fully deceived in some aspect of our lives.

When we are not being blessed financially, when we are experiencing major disappointments in life, when our expectations are dashed, we will begin to (consciously or subconsciously) question whether God loves us. The fear of God not loving us reinforces pride and self-reliance. We will not depend on God if we do not believe He loves us. Believers who deal with false adequacy are not sure if God loves them, and often are not sure how much they love God. If we have been doing life our own way, we may even possess some fear about talking to God.

We all operate with preconceived notions about why God blesses one person or another. People who have false adequacy do not understand why God blesses other people but not them. They are always looking at the blessings of others and saying things like, "She doesn't deserve that. She doesn't even go to church." Our desire to receive the blessings of God tends to make us favor works over grace. We perform the deeds we believe will cause God to favor us. This reinforces an insecurity about who God will bless and why.

When a believer with false adequacy is forced to pray, he may minimize his need for God. One man declared, "I don't pray to God about the little stuff; I work most things out myself." Another man prayed, "Lord, if You just answer this one little prayer, I won't bother You for a while." Both of these statements are a reflection of someone living his life at a religious distance from the Father. The false adequacy is made apparent in the words that show they don't believe they need much of God. They would like for Him to be handy when they are in a bind. However, getting to know God, submitting to Him and relying fully on Him, is far from their thoughts.

Overconfidence

One of the greatest signs of false adequacy is overconfidence. God's way is always the way of humility, but the devil's way is that of overconfidence and pride. Overconfidence is giving ourselves credit for having already accomplished something that we have not yet mastered. Overconfidence is the false view that we have come this far in life by our own strength, intellect, wisdom or gifts.

False adequacy is rampant among today's youth. From an early age, the enemy works to convince young people that they have no need for God or His guidance. The enemy's success in this area is evidenced by their rejection of education, rejection of morals, and choice of alternative lifestyles. Overly impressed with themselves, our youth embrace their own reasoning, and consequently, the reasoning of the enemy. This false adequacy breeds rebellion against parents. It can also lead children to join gangs or engage in debauchery.

When a person has false adequacy, he is not able to tell his rank among other people. He is like a brand new private in the military who is given the privilege of driving the general to a meeting. The private enters the room full of high-ranking military officials and because he has not yet learned rank, he strolls around running off at the mouth, never realizing how out of sync he is with the chain of command. This private has only been enlisted for two weeks, yet he is going around giving his superiors his opinion and telling them about changes he thinks need to be made. His overconfidence is evident to everyone but himself. This is a picture of our youth today—overconfident about life, in need of instruction, and full of false adequacy!

Rejection of People

False adequacy leads us to believe that life is all about us and that other people matter less than we do—or not at all. Many believers would quickly respond to this by saying, "I never feel like I am better than other people," but such belief often secretly resides in the hearts of people. For example, a poor man can believe he is "better" than a rich man if the rich man is unsaved. This poor man may be better off for being saved, but in the scheme of life, many would say he is not better because of his financial lack. There is a great danger in believing we are "better than" another person simply because we are better off financially, or of another race, or because we have a relationship with God. False adequacy causes us to resist certain people and situations we consider to be beneath us. We strive to associate only with people who meet our standards of acceptance. Those standards may be "saved" or "wealthy" or "intelligent" or "successful" or "spiritual" or "knowledgeable of the Bible," or any other thing. The point is, false adequacy makes whatever we believe is special about us, the criteria for our acceptance of others. In this way, false adequacy causes us to look down on other people.

Many believers who deal with false adequacy have difficulty finding a church home. They may claim they cannot find the right fit, but the real reason is because they arrogantly believe they are better than other saints. They are often guilty of saying things like, "I can't go to this church because they don't preach the Word," or "I don't go to that church because they are not what they should be." Then they sit at home and become their own pastor, watching religious services on television, yet never worshipping or being accountable to God. They are impressed with themselves, while looking down on the imperfections of God's people. They fail to realize that they are just as spiritually sick as those upon whom they are passing judgment. Jesus was humble enough to fellowship with sinners (Mark 2:15), but many believers have rejected the saints because of false adequacy.

Those who deal with false adequacy often value their gifts above the Body of Christ. Their spiritual or natural gifts become more important to them than God's people. Impressed with their giftedness, they feel they are to be preferred above other believers. False adequacy makes us strive to be independent of others and can be identified by the refusal to integrate or collaborate with other believers. False adequacy overemphasizes the "you need me" side of relationships, but has little appreciation for the "I need you" side. Those with false adequacy strive to prove to themselves, and to others, that all they need is God. They feel that as long as they have God, they don't need anyone else. These believers advocate a sort of "Lone Ranger Christianity" where they are the hero bringing God to everyone else. However, nothing could be further from the truth. God made us with limitations and weaknesses so that we would rely on one another.

We cannot have a solid marriage until false adequacy is broken over our lives. Marriage is the union of two people who realize that they are inadequate without one another. Marriage is one of the first principles of prosperity, a requirement many believers must fulfill if they are to see financial increase. One of the keys to a solid marriage is to be deeply convinced that you need your spouse. A person consumed by false adequacy still desperately needs a partner in life, but insists on believing that he is doing fine as a single individual. The tenuousness of today's marriages suggests that most modern-day believers are not convinced that they truly need their spouse. False adequacy deludes one into believing that his/her spouse is optional.

False adequacy causes us to become offended by the suggestion that we need the help of others. False adequacy causes us to resist the input of other people in our lives. We want to be able to do life on our own. We want to prosper on our own. We accept the fact that we need God, but in reality, we even minimize our need for God.

In the Old Testament, God made Israel submit to the Gentiles because of their arrogance.

And it shall come to pass, that the nation and kingdom which will not serve the same Nebuchadnezzar the king of Babylon, and that will not put their neck under the yoke of the king of Babylon, that nation will I punish, saith the Lord, with the sword, and with the famine, and with the pestilence, until I have consumed them by his hand.

Therefore hearken not ye to your prophets, nor to your diviners, nor to your dreamers, nor to your enchanters, nor to your sorcerers, which speak unto you, saying, Ye shall not serve the king of Babylon:

For they prophesy a lie unto you, to remove you far from your land; and that I should drive you out, and ye should perish.

But the nations that bring their neck under the yoke of the king of Babylon, and serve him, those will I let remain still in their own land, saith the Lord; and they shall till it, and dwell therein.

Jeremiah 27:8-11

To break the power of false adequacy in our lives, God has to do the same to us today by requiring us to submit to people and situations that we may view as beneath us. Many believers fail to realize that "relying on God" often looks a lot different than they thought. Relying on God can mean allowing someone else to teach us. Relying on God can mean asking our neighbor for a ride. Relying on God can mean asking someone to help us. Our pride often backs us into a corner as we assume we understand the ways and means of God. We reject the help of people, and then assume God will help us. Other people are often the tools God uses to help us accomplish His will. Paul the Apostle was a great man of God who accomplished many things, but he could not have done it without Barnabas, Ananias, Aquila and Priscilla, Silas, Timothy, Titus, and many others.

For years, I entertained thoughts of greatness that were rooted in pride and arrogance. My longing for greatness was evidenced by my lack of appreciation for the ministries of other men of God. I assumed that my knowledge of the Word and my gift to teach made me better than other ministers. I did not consciously say out of my mouth that I was better than them, but the evidence of my arrogance was in my failure to fellowship with these men and women of God.

My goal was to be successful, have a mega-church, and show others that I was God's man. Instead, I should have been thankful that God would allow a broken sinner like me to be saved, made righteous, and called a man of God. The Body of Christ is fragmented today because of false adequacy. Many ministers are starstruck with ideas of greatness precipitated by false adequacy. It is time that we realize that God is not interested in glorifying us; God is interested in glorifying Himself. And He is the only One worthy of the glory!

When we allow false adequacy into our lives, God has no choice but to allow life to convince us of our inadequacy. Today, many saints are on the humbling block in the plan of God. God is waiting for them to come to the realization that they desperately need Him in their lives. He is waiting for them to remove the distance between Him and them.

In reality, all of our efforts at life apart from God are meaningless. I recently heard a song that encouraged us by saying, when you don't know what to do, call on God. The truth is, we never know what to do. It is about time we stop trying to be the shepherd of our own lives and be content to be sheep!

Chapter 2

The Pride that Hides

There is a pride that comes out of the mind, which we refer to as arrogance. There is a pride that comes out of the will, which we refer to as stubbornness. And finally, there is a pride that proceeds forth from the heart; this we refer to as rebellion.

The pride that comes out of the heart is the pride that makes us rebel against God. This is the pride that God has to deliver us from. We can be destitute of material possessions and still be full of pride in our heart.

If God tells us to do something but we do what we want to do instead, we are full of pride. The book of Hebrews refers to this kind of heart as, *"an evil heart of unbelief"* (Hebrews 3:12). This simply means that we want to live our lives our own way.

Maybe you have met someone who didn't want to admit that he was wrong, even though the fact that he was wrong was so obvious. Or perhaps, you met someone who knew the right thing to do in a situation, but refused to do it just to spite someone. In both instances, internal pride or pride of the heart is present.

As a young minister, I sought after knowledge. Since I had a teaching gift, I specifically wanted to increase my knowledge of the Bible. I erroneously believed that success in ministry would come solely as the result of my own intellect. I thought that if I had more knowledge than other ministers, I would deservedly achieve more success. However, while growing in knowledge of the Word, I neglected to develop any other pastoral skills. My own drive for success through knowledge had become a source of inner pride. I had set my own course in life and was determined to achieve success!

Sincerely Wrong!

There's a difference between "sincerity" and the "will of God." Just because we are sincere does not necessarily imply that we are in the will of God. Too often, instead of asking God if what we are doing is His will, we will conduct a "sincerity check." For instance, during the first twenty years of my ministry, I was sincere in my love for God even though I was walking in pride. I was *sincerely* doing things my own way and was angry with God because He was not blessing my plans. *I was sincerely wrong!* My sincerity did not guarantee that God agreed with what I was doing.

Walking the streets of Union Springs, Alabama, during that time when I did not have an automobile humbled me. I liken it to the revelation that dawned on the prodigal son when he was feeding swine in the far country (Luke 15:11-32). It was during this season in my life that someone asked me a simple question, "Whose church is it—yours or God's?"

I had given little thought to whether the things I did in the church were pleasing to God. For years, I had run the church based on my intellectual design. Yet, as I pondered this question, I began to realize that for years I had called Jesus "Lord," but had not conducted myself as if He actually was my Lord. Sadly, many pastors today don't believe or act as if Jesus Christ is the owner of their ministry. Everything we do as pastors in our church must have Christ's approval—from sermons to pastoral appointments, right down to what we wear on Sunday morning!

An Unbroken Will

Pride results when we fail to fully submit to the will of God. In other words, pride is a by-product of an unbroken will. If our will is not broken, we are standing on the principle of pride. Often the trials we experience are a result of our unbroken will. I have heard people say, "I have been through hell, but my will remains unbroken." We will never fully submit to the will of God until our will is completely broken.

You may ask, "What does a broken will look like?" Someone with a broken will is bound and determined to do nothing with his life except what God wants him to do. As long our will stays intact, the will of God will be subject to our plans and pursuits. We can be in a very humbling circumstance and still be proud. Sometimes circumstances that come our way are actually opportunities for us to humble ourselves. If we choose to humble ourselves in these instances, God can elevate us. But too often instead of humbling ourselves, we grind our way through life resisting God, determined to do things our own way.

Mental Trophies

When we accomplish or achieve things in life, we must remember that it's by the grace of God. For instance, His grace allows us to get an education, start a business or be successful in any field of endeavor. Yet too often, like King Nebuchadnezzar, we give ourselves credit for what God has done in our lives. Earthly accomplishments can be a great source of pride.

Let's take a look at the story of King Nebuchadnezzar found in Daniel 4:29-33. King Nebuchadnezzar looked up and saw what had been accomplished during his tenure as king and pride rose up in his heart.

At the end of twelve months (Nebuchadnezzar) walked in the palace of the kingdom of Babylon. The king spake, and said, Is not this great Babylon, that I have built for the house of the kingdom by the might of my power, and for the honor of my majesty? While the word was in the king's mouth, there fell a voice from heaven, saying O king Nebuchadnezzar, to thee it is spoken; thy kingdom is departed from thee. And they shall drive thee from men, and thy dwelling shall be with the beast of the field: they shall make thee to eat grass as oxen, and seven times shall pass over thee, until thou know that the Most High ruleth in the kingdom of men, and giveth it to whomsoever he will. The same hour was the thing fulfilled upon Nebuchadnezzar: and he was driven from men, and did eat grass as oxen, and his body was wet with the dew of heaven, till his hairs were grown like eagles feathers, and his nails like birds' claws.

(explanation mine)

Daniel 5:17-21 further illustrates how King Nebuchadnezzar's heart was lifted up with pride.

Then Daniel answered and said before the king, Let thy gifts be to thyself, and give thy rewards to another; yet I will read the writing unto the king, and make known to him the interpretation. O thou king, THE MOST HIGH GOD GAVE Nebuchadnezzar thy father a kingdom, and majesty and glory and honor. And for the majesty that he gave him, all people, nations, and languages, trembled and feared before him: whom he would slay: and whom he would kept alive; and whom he would he set up; and whom he would he put down. But when HIS HEART WAS LIFTED UP, and his mind hardened in PRIDE, he was deposed from his kingly throne, and they took his glory from him. And he was driven from the sons of men; and his heart was made like the beasts, and his dwelling was with the wild asses: they fed him with grass like oxen, and his body was wet with the dew of heaven; till he knew that the most high God ruled in the kingdom of men, and that he appointeth over it whomsoever he will.

(emphasis mine)

Inner pride comes in many forms. Many of us are sweet and compassionate on the exterior, yet full of mental trophies. A mental trophy is something that we deem as important or something in life that we believe gives us significance. Anything in our lives that we pursue to the neglect of God's will is a mental trophy.

Self-perception can be a mental trophy we carry around. If we see ourselves as upper class, it may affect how we view others. Our desire to associate with the upper class can become an idol in our lives. In my personal life, my education did not make me proud in the classic sense of looking down on people, but when I had to move into a low income apartment, my self-perception skewed my opinion of those around me. I couldn't relate to my neighbors because I saw them as "uneducated," while I saw myself as "educated" or upper class. I convinced myself that I did not think I was better than my neighbors, I was just different, but this still was a mental trophy I carried with me.

The need to be important among people can also be a mental trophy. For instance, consider people who are unwilling to go into a thrift store and buy clothes or other necessities when that is all they can afford. They say it's because they don't want to wear other people's clothing; truthfully, this is just a form of personal pride.

When we have a need in life but resist the provision of God because it does not come in the form that sets well with our mental trophies, we are in pride. For example, I knew a certain believer who was a college graduate. She went to school to become a teacher but after she graduated, she could not find employment as a teacher, so she had to go work for a telemarketing company. She believed that since she had a college degree, she should have distinction from the other employees in the company. These feelings made it difficult for her to embrace, receive, and relax around her fellow employees. When the other employees carried on conversations in the break room, she would interrupt them by saying, "I don't know about you all, but I won't be here long. I am a teacher." She was too busy resenting God for her "low status" job and so disgruntled about having to work with "inferiors," that she never gave thanks to God for blessing her with a job in a tough economy.

This is the sort of pride we need to get rid of in our lives! We need to humble ourselves and get free from these mental trophies.

The Pride of Being Saved

Pride is much more than the idea of walking around with our noses in the air and our heads on a swivel. For many people, the only type of pride they know is social arrogance so whenever the word "pride" is mentioned, they conjure up images of prejudice and inflated social significance. But many saints today are full of pride, though it is not the overt pride that registers as arrogance. It is the internal pride that resides in our will and causes us to live our lives independent from God. It's the pride within us that only the Holy Spirit can expose.

Pride comes from the flesh so even though we are born again, we can still generate pride because we are living in fleshly bodies. There is a pride that comes from being saved that can completely derail our lives. We can be proud that we are saved and then because of that pride, distance ourselves from other people—both saved and unsaved.

The pride that comes from being saved manifests itself in different ways. For one person, this kind of pride may cause them to look down on or judge the unsaved. For another person, that same pride may cause him to refuse to go to work because he believes that God is obligated to take care of him. For yet another person, the pride of being saved may cause him to declare that he is the only one going to heaven.

For me personally, this pride gave me the false pretense that I did not need others. Therefore, I lived my life with a false sense of adequacy and distanced myself from others. This is also known as spiritual arrogance.

Stubbornness

Stubbornness is also a form of pride. When we are stubborn, we trust ourselves more than we trust God. We insist on having our own way. There is a prideful spirit that manifests in the attitude of *I am never wrong* or, *This is my life and I know what is best for me.*

If you are already proud in your heart as a poor person, what will you be if God blesses you financially? So often, we associate pride with money or status, but there are many people who are hindered by pride who have neither money nor status.

Meekness

The definition of meekness is sensitivity to God's voice and submission to His will. The absence of meekness in the life of a believer indicates that there is a presence of pride.

Meekness does not mean weakness; meekness is strength under control. The best analogy I have found for meekness is that of two horses in a field. One horse is wild, and the other horse has been tamed. Standing out grazing in the field, both horses appear the same. However, the difference between the two horses comes to light when the master tries to impose his will on the animals. One horse obediently submits while the other horse provides rank resistance. Is one horse stronger than the other? No. One has learned to submit, while the other has not.

We see the same scene played out in believers in the church. One is there to learn and submit to God, while the other is there to only graze, not submit to or obey God's voice. God knows the level of our submission. Some believers have shown a small amount of meekness by submitting to the Cross for salvation. Yet many are still walking in their imaginations and in the pride of this life. God does not accept half-trained horses. We must die to ourselves fully if we want to be used by God.

Humility

Many times, disobedience is the result of pride. The modern mind has dismissed pride as a possible reason why our lives are displeasing to God. But 1 Peter 5:5 tells us to, *"be clothed with humility."* What a powerful metaphor! Just as our bodies are to be covered in clothing, so are we to walk in humility. The passage goes on to offer several powerful references to pride and its antithesis, humility.

God resists the proud, and giveth grace to the humble. Humble yourselves therefore under the mighty hand of God, that he may exalt you in due time.

1 Peter 5:5-6

God resists the proud. This is why we must humble ourselves! I must announce to you that God is expecting you to do the humbling. You are to examine yourself, identify pride within you, and eradicate it. When was the last time you humbled yourself? I have had experiences in my life where if I had just been humble, I would not have been put to shame.

Pride goes before destruction and a haughty spirit before a fall.

Proverbs 16:18

We can be in a very humbling situation and yet not humble ourselves. Then there are people who are only superficially humble. They put on a veneer of humility when they experience humbling circumstances in their lives. However, the moment their circumstances change, their pride surges forth and they return to honoring their own opinions and once again become resistant to God.

God is seeking to bring us to a place of resignation where we declare, "Lord, I resign my gifts, my ability, my intelligence, my ideas, my life and I humbly accept Your will and plan for my life."

And thou shalt remember all the way which the LORD thy God led thee these forty years in the wilderness, TO HUMBLE THEE, and to prove thee, to know what was in thine heart, whether thou wouldest keep his commandments, or no. AND HE HUMBLED THEE, and suffered thee to hunger, and fed thee with manna, which thou knewest not, neither did thy fathers know: that he might make thee to know that man doth not live by bread only, but by every word that proceedeth out of the mouth of the LORD *doth man live…Who fed thee in the wilderness with manna, which thy fathers knew not, that HE MIGHT HUMBLE THEE, and that he might prove thee, to do thee good at the latter end.*

Deuteronomy 8:2-3, 16 (emphasis mine)

God is looking for humble people to bless. We can have a desperate need and still be too proud to receive from God. We need to humble ourselves and ask God to help us. As a baby is dependent upon his mother for milk, so must we be dependent upon our Heavenly Father. We must humble ourselves so God can take care of us.

Pride is frowned upon from a social perspective. We do not want others to say we are proud. Therefore, most of us embrace a certain amount of social humility. But we can be socially humble while being internally proud and resistant to the voice of God. Social humility is not what God is looking for. He is looking for an inner humility that is characterized by a life lived in dependency upon and obedience to Him.

God must break the pride of self-sufficiency in our lives. One of the biggest challenges we face is to be humble once we have noticed our gifts and talents that make us stand out. However, our gifts and talents should not be sources of pride, but rather impetus for gratitude and humility.

When we are proud, we work hard to control how others view us. When we are humble, we are comfortable with our lot in life. At one point in my life, I found it difficult to admit to myself that I was poor. A poor person can be humble on the exterior but still proud in his heart. I made choices and decisions that were inconsistent with my financial reality. I was poor and needed to humble myself and act like it, but instead, I resisted that label to my own peril. I didn't realize that being poor did not mean that I was not blessed. By the world's standard I was poor, but by God's standard, I am always blessed!

When I humbled myself and came to terms with my reality of being poor, it took a lot of stress out of my life. Jesus did not have a problem with the word "poor." In fact, He said, *"The poor you will always have with you"* (Mark 14:7).

We can be humbled by the fact that God has saved us, but proud in other areas of our lives. In Daniel 5:20, the Bible speaks of a person's heart being lifted up:

> *But when his heart was lifted up, and his mind hardened in pride, he was deposed from his kingly throne, and they took his glory from him.*

A person whose heart is lifted up may not have an external show of pride. Pride can be very deceptive. We are proud if we are not teachable, if we refuse instruction. We are proud if we always insist that our opinion is right. There are many people who are homeless and down on their luck, and the reason they do not reach out to God is because of internal pride. They are still trying to prove that they can "make it on the streets" rather than admit to God that they have messed up their lives.

Hezekiah: Pride & Prosperity

> *Thus the LORD saved Hezekiah and the inhabitants of Jerusalem from the hand of Sennacherib the king of Assyria, and from the hand of all other, and guided them on every side. And many brought gifts unto the LORD to Jerusalem, and presents to Hezekiah king of Judah; so that he was magnified in the sight of all nations from thenceforth. In those days Hezekiah was sick to the death, and prayed unto the*

LORD: *and he spake unto him, and he gave him a sign. But Hezekiah rendered not again according to the benefit done unto him; for his HEART WAS LIFTED UP: therefore there was wrath upon him and upon Judah and Jerusalem. Notwithstanding Hezekiah HUMBLED HIMSELF for the pride of his heart, both he and the inhabitants of Jerusalem, so that the wrath of the LORD came not upon them in the days of Hezekiah.*

2 Chronicles 32:22-26 (emphasis added)

In modern times, we don't think much of our pride. It is almost like we prefer to believe that pride no longer exists. For many believers, pride is a thing of the past, relegated to biblical times. Yet today, pride is one of the major reasons why God cannot endow many believers with prosperity. Many saints are praying and sowing seeds for prosperity, but God cannot bless the proud.

Let's consider King Hezekiah. In 2 Chronicles chapter thirty-two, King Hezekiah is embroiled with Sennacherib the king of Assyria. When we read this chapter, we get the sense that King Hezekiah recognized his inadequacy in the way that he encouraged his people to pray and call upon the Lord.

And for this cause Hezekiah the king, and the prophet Isaiah the son of Amoz, prayed and cried to heaven.

2 Chronicles 32:20

Thus the LORD saved Hezekiah and the inhabitants of Jerusalem from the hand of Sennacherib the king of Assyria.

2 Chronicles 32:22

God did what only God can do. He brought salvation and deliverance for Hezekiah and the people. However, many people miss the next part of the story. The biblical account says that *after* God delivered King Hezekiah and Israel from the king of Assyria, many people brought gifts to God and Hezekiah, and Hezekiah's name was heralded among the people. Through this prayer-wrenched deliverance, Hezekiah went from utter fear and potential failure to imminent success. This success was the real test for Hezekiah.

Many believers have handled failure for a long time, but very few have the grace to handle success. Are you humble enough to handle success? If God grants you to be exalted among men, will you direct glory to yourself or will you remember that it was God who brought you the victory? Do you tell people that God blessed you to live in a nice house or do you speak of how you worked hard to get where you are today? If you are a supervisor on your job, do you treat others with respect, remembering that it was God who promoted you—not man?

In the text from 2 Chronicles, there is a very odd sequence. Verse 23 says that Hezekiah was lauded and magnified among the people, then verse 24 says that he was sick unto death. What happened between verses 23 and 24 that caused such a drastic change? The story goes on to reveal that it was Hezekiah's pride that led to the malady. After God brought victory into Hezekiah's life, his pride resurged and he forgot the things God had done for him. Hezekiah was "sick unto death." In other words, he was actively dying.

The story goes on to say that Hezekiah *"prayed unto the LORD"* (2 Chronicles 32:24). There are many people who have left this earth because they were too proud to cry out to God, but instead said foolish things like, "I guess it is just my time to go." Pride makes an individual not want to acknowledge his need for God's assistance.

The scripture says that during Hezekiah's sickness, God spoke to him and gave him a sign. God was gracious to Hezekiah, doing more for him than was required. We can extrapolate that Hezekiah was fully healed, but he soon returned to his former prideful state of mind.

Hezekiah rendered not again according to the benefit done unto him; for his heart was lifted up.

2 Chronicles 32:25

Hezekiah came off of his death bed by the hand of God, but did not acknowledge or praise God for what He had done. He simply went on his way, leading people to believe that he did not die because of his own greatness. Hezekiah's pride was in his heart. Pride that's in the heart is often undetectable. Many people who seem like the picture of humility are actually proud in their heart. But God sees our pride, even if others do not.

Today many believers are like Hezekiah. We pray and ask God for something and then after we receive it, fail to give God acknowledgement for the gift. God does not take our failure to "render" lightly. The scripture says that there was wrath upon Hezekiah because of this omission. Second Chronicles 32:26 says that Hezekiah eventually recognized his error and *"humbled himself, for the pride of his heart."*

Second Chronicles 32:26 goes on to say that not only did Hezekiah humble himself, but all the inhabitants of Jerusalem humbled themselves. They were all consumed with pride! Think about people in your own life. Your company can be full of pride. Your school can be full of pride. Your neighborhood can be full of pride. Your church can be full of pride. Pride is a hindrance to God's blessing and favor—so let's humble ourselves and get rid of it!

Hezekiah's Prosperity

And Hezekiah had exceeding much riches and honor: and he made himself treasuries for silver, and for gold, and for precious stones, and for spices, and for shields, and for all manner of pleasant jewels; storehouses also for the increase of corn, and wine, and oil; and stalls for all manner of beast, and cotes for flocks. Moreover he provided him cities, and possessions of flocks and herds in abundance: for God had given him substance very much.

2 Chronicles 32:27-29

After Hezekiah humbled himself before God, the Lord did not hold his season of pride against him. Verses twenty-seven through twenty-nine begin the litany of Hezekiah's prosperity. God wants to prosper His people, but He will not prosper the proud.

Today, I am prospering more than I have in all my life and my finances are not coming from the church at all. God has truly shown me that He is faithful. When I humbled myself, God began to connect me to the blessing and I began to praise Him and give Him the glory for my prosperity.

It's time that we all check ourselves before God. It's time that we go before the Lord and say, "Lord, show me my pride." God is faithful to show us our sins and our pride if we ask Him. Then we must ask God to give us the spirit of humility that Jesus had. When the world sees that we have humbled ourselves before our God, they will also see the hand of God upon us and the prosperity of God among us. Hezekiah humbled himself—and so can we!

Chapter 3

God's Strength vs. Your Strength

We must come to the humbling realization that in all things in life, we are either operating in our own strength or in God's strength. There is no middle ground. For what we do in our own strength, we get the glory. For those things done in God's strength, He gets the glory. God will not comingle strengths.

One of the main reasons that so few believers have tapped into God's strength is because they haven't been convinced that they need it. God is the One who provides strength for all we do. Strength is of God.

He giveth power to the faint; and to them that have no might he increaseth strength.

Isaiah 40:29

Let's take a look at the topic of salvation. Either we are saved by the shed blood of Jesus Christ on Calvary, or we are still trying to earn salvation in our own strength. To have faith that Jesus' death on the Cross saves us is to put our confidence in God's strength. To have faith in our ability to save ourselves is to put our confidence in our own strength. The Cross and grace are God's strength; the law and works are man's strength. We cannot comingle God's plan of salvation with works and say, "I am saved through Jesus Christ, but I still have to earn my salvation by my good works."

For by grace are ye saved through faith; and that not of yourselves: it is the gift of God: Not of works, lest any man should boast.

Ephesians 2:8-9

God wants us to operate in His strength, not our own. The failure to understand this can result in a catastrophic Christian experience. Although Jesus was God incarnate and dying on the Cross was God's will for Him, even Jesus relied on the strength of God to accomplish the task.

And there appeared an angel unto him from heaven, strengthening him.

Luke 22:43

Jesus had to receive divine strength to do the assignment that God had for His life. Before going to the Cross, He prayed:

Nevertheless, not my will, but thine, be done.

Luke 22:42

One of the greatest idols in our life today is the desire to see our own will and design for our lives manifested. God, however, calls us to abandon our will, plan, and design completely for the sake of His will.

Without Him, We Can Do Nothing

When I say "your strength," I am referring to your abilities or your power. "Your strength" may mean your intellectual strength, your physical strength, your wisdom, your wit, your charisma, your beauty, your connections, your resources, your friends, your love, your kindness, or your ability to manipulate. Anything about you that you believe is capable of bringing about your own success in life is "your strength."

Many believers are still not convinced that Jesus was right when He said, *"Without me ye can do nothing"* (John 15:5). They are daily striving to bring about a certain condition or result for themselves that does not have the endorsement of God. For example, a Christian lady from our church was living in an apartment with a rent far above her income level. She had always dreamed of living in that part of the city but because the apartment was so expensive, she went without furniture and sometimes even without food. Yet, she was very proud to tell others where she lived.

After living in this apartment for about a year, she lost her job. She did not want to give up her apartment so she spent many hours in prayer and happened to call on me for counsel. She told me the reason she didn't want to leave her apartment was because it represented the life she built for herself, and now she felt like God wanted to take it away from her. In other words, that apartment represented her kingdom and her strength. I told her that it did not represent God well for her to fight with the apartment managers when she was behind on her rent. She declined to heed my counsel and refused to get out of the apartment, despite pending litigation. She remained committed to building her kingdom, even if it meant that she would fail to render any offering to God. She was set on living out her own will in her own strength.

For this woman, that apartment represented her strength; for others, it may be finding a spouse or getting rich in their own strength. Often, we would rather have a fantasy of what life could be if we live in our own strength, than have a blessed reality relying on God's strength. For example, many Christians would rather drive a twenty-year-old car in their own strength than drive a brand new car in the strength of God. They are stubbornly committed to proving they can do it on their own.

Whenever we are committed to building our own kingdom, God is limited in what He can do in our lives. When we rely on our strength, we do life our way. When we do life our way, we are out of God's will. When we are out of God's will, we are out of the favor of God.

A fundamental difference between modern-day believers and those who lived during New Testament times is that believers during New Testament times had a deeper understanding that their lives belonged to God. They understood that God was the King and they were His servants. The early Church was convinced of its need for God. When Jesus ascended, He turned the responsibility for representing God over to the Church. His first words of instruction were, *"Go and wait for the promise of the Father"* (Acts 1:4). He further says:

> *But ye shall receive power after that the Holy Ghost is come upon you, and ye shall be witnesses unto me both in Jerusalem, and in Judea, and in Samaria, and unto the uttermost part of the earth.*
>
> Acts 1:8

Jesus was basically saying, "You don't have what you need to be effective witnesses right now. You are inadequate! But the Father will give you His power to witness." He told them to wait for the coming of the Holy Spirit, who would provide the power to witness. The book of Acts depicts a Church so reliant on God that they spent a lot of time in prayer. They pleaded for God's power.

Today, we have many substitutes for the power of God—money, intelligence, strategies, technology, tradition, plans, and committees. All of these things give us a false sense of adequacy and deceive us into believing that we have gotten beyond the need for God's presence and power. Our prayerlessness is a reflection of our false sense of adequacy. When our preaching is bad, we go to school to learn how to preach. When our church is not growing, we read a book on church growth. Prayer is a last resort, if we turn to it at all.

Modern-day believers do not view God as the King of their lives, but rather as their personal assistant. Many have abandoned the responsibility for being servants to God and have made God servant to man. In their minds, the purpose of God is to help them live out the life that they have chosen for themselves. Consequently, they don't feel much of a sense of responsibility or accountability to God. They view their time, talents, and finances as their own, therefore, they live their lives unto themselves.

This generation will have to be delivered from the "Celebrity Christian" syndrome that is unique to the modern era. In today's world, being gifted and anointed means money, status, and glory, but this was not the case in past generations. Generations ago, being a servant of Jesus Christ meant living a selfless life, forsaking this world for the one to come. It meant a life of self-effacement and decrease so that God would get all the glory.

Unless we recalibrate our minds, we will continue to assume we have a right to the glory. Many of God's people are pimping the anointing. They take the anointing that God has put on their lives and use it for their own glory. When we deal with false adequacy, God has to turn down grace on our lives to keep us from taking the credit for what His anointing is doing. Many of us have had our goals and plans hindered by the Lord because they were rooted in a selfish pride. They were plans to glorify self, not God.

Today, I don't want to impress people; I want to impact people. I want to impact them with the gospel in such a way that it leaves them worshipping God. If we minister and people become more impressed with us, we are not glorifying God. The true servant of God is determined to bring the Father as much glory as possible. God must increase and we must decrease. Without Him —we are nothing! Once we come to this realization, praise, worship, and thanksgiving will take on a new meaning. It becomes the centerpiece of our ministry.

Humble Yourself

The first step to humbling ourselves is to get delivered from our own sense of adequacy. Then, we must become aware of God's adequacy. Our God is El Shaddai; He is the All-Sufficient One. This means that He is very capable of accomplishing anything and everything that we need. It is time to believe and confess that our God is able!

Relying on our own strength leads to a very limited life. It means staying in our comfort zone and continuing to do things based on our own reasoning. What we are "good at" and what we "like to do" can be an expression of things done in our strength.

The Apostle Paul had an impediment in his life. When he realized that he could not overcome it, he called upon the Lord. The Lord's words to Paul were:

MY GRACE is sufficient for thee: for MY STRENGTH is made perfect in weakness.

2 Corinthians 12:9 (emphasis mine)

This scripture tells us something very important. There is a strength of Paul, and there is a STRENGH of God! Paul had to learn to rely on God's strength. When you operate in your own strength, you are outside of the strength of God and disconnected from His will. Being outside of God's will guarantees disappointment. Many believers' lives are littered with hurts and disappointments that have mounted up over the years, creating soul wounds and bitterness generated from a life lived in their own strength.

As a student of the faith movement, I was taught for years about what God can do for me through faith. *"All things are possible to him who believes"* became the mantra of my life (Mark 9:23). However, after many years of being a part of the faith movement and being inundated with lessons about what God could do through faith, I came to realize there was another lesson that God had to teach me. That lesson concerned *what I cannot do in my strength.*

I realized that many things that I endeavored to do "by faith" were not of God, but of me. It was my strength that wrote the check, but I assumed God would sign it. Because my actions were not in line with God's will, I was operating in my own strength while claiming that I was acting in faith. At this point, I had not fully learned to submit to God. True reliance upon God means staying in communication with Him and asking Him to give you His will and His plan for your life, and then carrying out that plan by faith.

There are many believers who are walking "by faith," yet they are weary from a life lived in their own strength. If you are not living out God's perfect will for your life in God's perfect strength, then He is not obliged to honor your faith. He may offer some blessings simply because He is pleased with faith, but God's intention is to carry out His will for your life in His strength—not be a cosmic bell boy doing everything you can think of in faith.

For example, if you live in Texas and God wants you to move to New York, yet you strike out in the direction of California, you are out of God's will! You may pray, "Lord, protect me as I travel to California; Lord, give me favor to find good gas prices; Lord, I confess that I will have no mechanical problems on my journey; Lord, let me find the perfect place to live when I reach Los Angeles." But if God didn't tell you to go to California, your prayers will not be answered!

You many get offended with God because He did not answer your prayer. The enemy will begin to tell you that God is not listening to you and that the reason you are not being blessed is because of your sins. The reality is, you didn't check with God to find out His will for your life or you simply chose not to obey His will.

Moses' Strength

And Moses was learned in all the wisdom of the Egyptians, and was mighty in words and in deeds.

Acts 7:22

And seeing one of them suffer wrong, he defended him, and avenged him that was oppressed, and smote the Egyptian. For he supposed his brethren would have understood how that God by his hand would deliver them: but they understood not.

Acts 7:24-25

Moses was a man who had to learn how to rely on God's strength. From the very beginning, Moses' mother and father recognized that a special calling was upon his life (Exodus 2:2). He was called to be a deliverer. When Moses was fully grown, he perceived this calling himself and tapped into his life's purpose. He realized that he would be the man who would set the Hebrews free from their Egyptian bondage.

One day, Moses came out and saw one of the Egyptians beating a Hebrew slave and Moses killed the Egyptian. He sought to deliver the people in his own strength (Exodus 2:12-14). Moses was correct that he was the deliverer, but he was mistaken to believe that it would be his strength that would bring the deliverance. Moses had to learn how to yield to God's strength. It's the same way in our lives. Even though we may be anointed and gifted, if what we do is not done in God's will and in God's strength, it will not produce the desired results.

Our greatest strengths outside of God's will bring dismal results, and our greatest weaknesses within God's strength bring God's power for sweat-less victory. In our strength, we can make one million phone calls and get one dollar, but in God's strength, we can make one phone call and get one million dollars. That's a big difference!

In our world today, too many believers are operating in their own strength, just like Moses did. They love the Lord and their intentions are good, but they are going about the task in their own strength. Then when they get negative results, they give up and become angry with God and man. Just as Moses was not adequate to bring about the people's deliverance in his strength, we are not adequate to bring about results in our own lives by our strength.

The New Moses

Forty years later, we find Moses living in Midian. This is the same Moses—yet different. This Midianite shepherd is a humbled version of the man we knew back in Egypt. It is this new Moses that God chose to use to fulfill His purpose. When God spoke to him on the mountain, Moses recognized his inadequacy and said:

Who am I, that I should go unto Pharaoh, and that I should bring
forth the children of Israel out of Egypt.

Exodus 3:11

Moses was no longer the strong stud who tried to deliver Israel
with his bare hands. He had been humbled, so he no longer saw himself as adequate. Only in this humbled and self-aware state was Moses
useful to God. God's words to Moses were, *"Certainly, I will be with*
thee" (Exodus 3:12).

Peter's Strength

And saw two ships standing by the lake: but the fishermen were
gone out of them, and were washing their nets. And he entered
into one of the ships, which was Simon's and prayed him that he
would thrust out a little from the land. And he sat down, and
taught the people out of the ship. Now when he had left speaking,
he said unto Simon, Launch out into the deep, and let down your
nets for a draught. And Simon answering said unto him, 'Master,
we have toiled all the night, and have taken nothing: nevertheless,
AT THY WORD I will let down the net.

Luke 5:2-5 (emphasis mine)

Peter was a well-trained fisherman with many years of experience;
Jesus was a Jewish rabbi who, Peter assumed, did not know the lake
or the temperament of the fish. Yet, it was Jesus who told Peter to let
down his nets once again. Peter's response to Jesus was, *"But we have*
toiled all night and caught nothing." Peter might have added, "And Jesus,
what do You know about fishing?"

Peter struggled within himself with Jesus' request, because his
knowledge of fishing was vast. Yet, despite his knowledge, he could

not bring about the results he desired. Jesus was attempting to assist Peter, if Peter was humble enough to receive the assistance.

Notice that Peter's words were, *"we have toiled all night."* One of the signs that someone is in their own strength is that they "toil." When we are out of the will of God, we have stress and worry and have to force things to happen. When we operate in our own strength, we simply get tired. We grow weary, disappointed, and angry with God. The Christian life is not designed to make us tired, weary, worn out, frustrated, depressed, or angry. When we are working in our own strength, we fail to realize that what we are toiling for, God actually wants to give us.

Peter was operating in his own strength, but Jesus wanted Peter to rely on Him. Peter switched from his own strength to God's strength when he declared, *"Nevertheless, at thy word."* The phrase "at thy word" implies a life lived according to God's will. When we set out to do ministry, work, relationships, or life without God's direction, we are destined to toil!

Not by might, nor by power, but by my Spirit says the LORD.
Zechariah 4:6

He that has entered into his rest, he also hath ceased from his own works.
Hebrews 4:10

As long as we are striving to reach our goals in our own strength, we will remain in the wilderness. Life is hard in the wilderness. However, when we resign to God's strength, we will have victory. God does not want to work *with* us; He wants to work *through* us.

The Prodigal Son

A certain man had two sons: And the younger of them said to his father, Father give me the portion of goods that falleth to me. And he divided unto them his living. And not many days after the younger son gathered all together, and took his journey into a far country, and there wasted his substance with riotous living. And when he had spent all, there arose a mighty famine in that land; and he began to be in want.

Luke 15:11-14

The prodigal son requested his inheritance from his father because he wanted to provide his own direction for his life. Being under the father's supervision had become boring; he wanted to get out and stretch his wings. When we provide the direction for our lives, we must also provide the strength to get it done. The reason we rely on our own strength is because we want to show ourselves, and others, that we are adequate. We want to show people we know how to do life. The reason many people delay in coming to God is because they want to prove that they can do life without Him, just as the prodigal son wanted to prove that he could do life without his father. Because the father knew how important it was for his son to learn the important life lesson that we cannot make it in our own strength, he obliged himself to give his son his inheritance.

There are some lessons in life that are better learned by experience. We may be better off without the experience, but the lesson still has to be learned. The prodigal son's motivation to go his own way was also influenced by inner sin. Within the young man was not only a desire to go his own way, but also a desire to live a life outside his father's rules.

The young man set out from his father's house in his own strength to do his own thing. So often, the reason many saints end up in their own strength is because they do not like God's commandments, plans, or ideas for their life. In an effort to rebel, they go their own way and do life in their own strength. As in the case of the prodigal son, so often this rebellion against God is fueled by one's own lust. The end result of the prodigal son's escapades was that he ended up broke and desolate.

When we find ourselves in this condition, we are often advised, "You need to get your life together." These misstatements send us deeper into the abyss of our own strength. From the hog pen, we strive to get our lives together—when it was our trying to get our lives together in our own strength that created the problem in the first place.

When our strength brings us low, we may be tempted to "fix it." However, any attempt on our part to "fix it" brings us into deeper reliance on our own strength and further away from the strength of God. This is a vicious cycle that leaves us resentful and angry with God. The enemy tells us that God does not love us or care about us.

The prodigal son made the right decision to abandon his own efforts and fully return home to his father. Perhaps if the prodigal son had found success in the far country, he might have continued with his sins and never returned home. Unfortunately, this is often the case with many believers. They are proud when things are going well, and humbled when they are not. When their clever ways are successful, they work their plans; when they find themselves in a pit, they get angry and discouraged and cry out to God. They never fully commit to live in the strength of God and so spend their lives in a half-hearted relationship with Him.

Our financial prosperity brings with it the temptation to do life in our own strength. This is what the Lord meant when he spoke through Jeremiah saying:

Thus saith the LORD; cursed be the man that trusteth in man, and maketh flesh his arm, and whose heart departeth from the LORD. For he shall be like the heath in the desert, and shall not see when good cometh; but shall inhabit the parched places in the wilderness in a salt land and not inhabited.

Jeremiah 17:5-6

We desperately want to believe in our own strength, therefore, if we get a glimmer of hope that our plans will work, we tend to distance ourselves from God. Then when we crash, we come running back to God! God cannot bless us when we are in our strength, so we need to make a decision to live life from His strength, submitting our entire life to Him, finding out His plans and ideas, and then walking in them.

There are many devices in a man's heart; nevertheless the counsel of the LORD, that shall stand.

Proverbs 19:21

Our plans must die, and God's plans must live. All of our plans must have the endorsement of God!

"Ishmael"

Now Sarai Abram's wife bare him no children: and she had an handmaid, an Egyptian, whose name was Hagar. And Sarai said unto Abram, behold now, the LORD hath restrained me from bearing: I pray thee, go in unto my maid; it may be that I may ob-

tain children by her. And Abram hearkened to the voice of Sarai. And Sarai, Abram's wife, took Hagar her maid the Egyptian, after Abram had dwelt ten years in the land of Canaan, and gave her to her husband Abram to be his wife...And Hagar bare Abram a son: and Abram called his son's name, which Hagar bare, Ishmael.

Genesis 16:1-3, 15

And Abraham said unto God, O that Ishmael might live before thee! And God said (to Abraham), Sarah thy wife shall bear thee a son indeed; and thou shall call his name Isaac: and I will establish my covenant with him.

Genesis 17:18-19 (explanation mine)

And Sarah saw the son of Hagar the Egyptian, which she had born unto Abraham, mocking. Wherefore she said unto Abraham, Cast out this bondwoman and her son: for the son of this bondwoman shall not be heir with my son, even with Isaac.

Genesis 21:9-10

In Abram's heart, there was nothing he desired more than to have a son. Because God knew this, He promised Abram that He would give him a son. Abram and Sarai received the promise by faith. But after years of waiting and wondering how and when God would bless them, they both began to doubt the promises of God. In their doubt and unbelief, they began to reason and waver. Instead of waiting for God's strength to bring about a divinely promised child, they resorted to human strength. Sarai, in her craftiness, figured out how she could turn the promise of God into a reality. She offered her handmaid Hagar to Abraham to be his wife so that she could, in turn, claim Hagar's child. Sarai's decision to operate in her own strength almost destroyed her marriage.

53

Abram and Sarai's story represents the tendency for us to "help God out." Nothing gets us out of faith and out of God's will faster than when we conclude that we need to help God do what He said He would do if we would only believe. Abram and Sarai produced "Ishmael" in their own strength. Ishmael represents what is not of God!

When we, in our strength, decide to "help God out," we show that we have not learned to trust God and take Him at His word. When we intervene and interfere with the plan of God, we mess things up! Many of the things we possess in our lives today are "Ishmaels." We might have achieved some results in our own strength, but it was not what God had in mind. Whatever is produced outside of God's strength is an Ishmael in our lives and will not please God.

There are people who have an Ishmael marriage; they have entered into covenant with someone who was not approved of by God. There are people who are working an Ishmael job; their job is not God's perfect will for their lives. There are people who have an Ishmael ministry; they have not been called to preach or they are ministering outside of God's assignment for their lives. Whatever is done without faith is an Ishmael:

Whatsoever is not of faith is sin.

Romans 14:23

Sarai gave Abram her handmaid because of her fear that she would never have children. Abram accepted Hagar because of his fear that he would not have an heir. When the enemy attacks with fear, he is hoping that we will panic and produce an Ishmael. Many of God's children today are producing and living with their Ishmaels, but it is high time to believe the promises of God. We can continue life in our own strength and have an Ishmael, or we can look to God for His strength and have an "Isaac." Let's choose the latter!

Samson: A Man of Strength

Most of us learned the story of Samson at a tender age. Children love to tell of his great strength. However, when we come to maturity, we must get one thing straight—Samson's human strength was small. It was God's strength that allowed Samson to enjoy victories over the Philistines.

> *And when (Samson) came unto Lehi, the Philistines shouted against him: and the Spirit of the LORD came mightily upon him, and the cords that were upon his arms became as flax that was burnt with fire, and his bands loosed from off his hands. And he found a new jawbone of an ass, and put forth his hand, and took it, and slew a thousand men.*
>
> Judges 15:14-15 (explanation mine)

We have talked much about the thousand men that Samson slew, however this scripture uses the phrase, *"And the Spirit of the LORD came mightily upon him..."* It was the Spirit of the Lord coming upon him that provided the strength to slay those thousand men.

Consider another occasion with Samson. *"Then went Samson down, and his father and his mother to Timnath, and came to the vineyards of Timnath: and behold, a young lion roared against him. And the Spirit of the LORD came mightily upon him, and he rent him as he would have rent a kid, and he had nothing in his hand"* (Judges 14:5-6). Again, it was the Spirit of the Lord that enabled Samson to overcome the lion.

> *And she made him sleep upon knees; and she called for a man, and she caused him to shave off the seven locks of his head; and she began to afflict him, and his strength went from him.*
>
> Judges 16:19

Samson's hair—or human strength—did not give him power over the Philistines or the lion. It was the strength of the Lord that gave Samson each of his victories. Samson's strength was not in his hair. His hair was merely a sign of his covenant with God and in order to keep that covenant, all Samson had to do was not allow his hair to be cut.

Samson broke his covenant with God by sharing his secrets with Delilah, which led to his hair being cut. Once Samson's hair was cut, his covenant with God was broken. At that point, Samson reverted to operating in his own strength. When Samson kept the covenant with God, he walked in an anointing of strength. However, when he broke covenant with God, he found his human strength was inadequate. Without the strength of God, Samson could do nothing—and neither can we!

Too often, we minister under the power of God but give ourselves the credit for the outcome, not realizing that without the imposition of the Spirit, we can do nothing. If we are obedient to God, we will be anointed by God, but when we are disobedient, we are out of step with God's power.

The world's philosophy is: *Never admit your weaknesses.* God's philosophy is: *Always know that you are powerless.* There is a pride that is manifested in wanting other people to view us as strong. But God remains unimpressed with human strength. To God, even our so-called strengths are weaknesses.

Many of us have had seasons of our lives when God has placed His grace on our human efforts. But today, God is calling us higher. He will no longer bless our strength. It is time we fully embrace God's strength.

Not by might, nor by power, but by my Spirit saith the LORD.

Zechariah 4:6

Finally, my brethren, be strong in the Lord and in the power of his might.

Ephesians 6:10

David

David was a praying man who was humble enough to check with God before he did anything. We have heard of prayers of intercession, thanksgiving, and supplication, yet David prayed prayers of inquiry. These prayers of inquiry petitioned God for information or understanding.

Call upon me, and I will answer you, and show you great and mighty things that you do not know.

Jeremiah 33:3

Our generation is lacking in the matter of praying prayers of inquiry. God promises to show us the things that we do not know, if we will only call upon Him. Once a believer comes to the humbling realization that he does not know it all, he may seek God for guidance. Until we are humble, we may pray prayers of intercession and supplication, but never prayers of inquiry. David was a man who was not impressed with his intellect or his abilities. He completely relied on God's strength.

Consider David's prayer life:

Therefore, David enquired of the LORD.

1 Samuel 23:2

Then David enquired of the LORD yet again.

1 Samuel 23:4

(David) said to Abiathar the priest, Bring hither the ephod. Then said David, O LORD God of Israel, thy servant hath certainly heard that Saul seeketh to come to Keilah, to destroy the city for my sake. Will the men of Keilah deliver me up into his hand? will Saul come down, as thy servant hath heard? O LORD God of Israel, I beseech thee, tell thy servant. And the LORD said, He will come down. Then said David, Will the men of Keilah deliver me and my men into the hand of Saul? And the LORD said, They will deliver thee up.

1 Samuel 23:9-12

And David enquired at the LORD, saying, shall I pursue after this troop? Shall I overtake them? And he (God) answered him, Pursue: for thou shalt surely overtake them, and without fail recover all.

1 Samuel 30:8 (explanation mine)

And it came to pass after this, that David enquired of the LORD, saying, Shall I go up into any of the cities of Judah? And the LORD said unto him, Go up. And David said, Whither shall I go up? And he said, Unto Hebron.

2 Samuel 2:1

And David enquired of the LORD saying, Shall I go up to the Philistines? Wilt thou deliver them into mine hand? And the LORD said unto David, Go up: for I will doubtless deliver the Philistines into thine hand.

2 Samuel 5:19

Get the picture? David was continually inquiring of the Lord in prayer, and we should do the same. When you get ready to purchase a new car, do you check with God and enquire as to what car God wants you to buy? When you meet someone you are interested in dating, do you check with God and enquire if it is the person He has in mind for you, or if it is time for you to date? Do you make decisions about life based on your intellect and then ask God to bless your decisions? Do you invite God into your choices in life?

When we check with God, we will know we are in His will, and He will lead us in the right path. It is a wonderful thing to go to a job interview knowing that God has told you in advance that this is the job He has for you. It is comforting to go on a date knowing that God has showed you that this is the man or woman He has ordained for your life. It is reassuring when you write a check, knowing that God told you to give.

This matter of praying prayers of inquiry or "checking with God" is very important if we want to be in God's will. We do not automatically know God's will. Often, God has to instruct us and direct us concerning His will. I should add that we must not take on the mentality that we will check with God only on the "big things" of life, such as when we purchase a home or when we desire to get married. Checking with God should become a daily activity that we do even in the smallest of matters.

This doesn't mean that we should be afraid to take a step in the morning without the direction of God. We don't need to stand in front of the refrigerator and say, "Lord, what do You want me to eat?" That would be excessive. However, we need to be prayerful and sensitive to the direction of the Holy Spirit, taking time to stop and pray about decisions that may seem inconsequential. Being led by the Spirit goes hand in hand with seeking God's direction through prayer. Jesus was led by the Holy Spirit, and He also spent much time in prayer.

Men of Gibeon

When the Israelites entered the Promised Land, they took the cities of Jericho and Ai. Not long after these victories, they came upon some Gibeonite men who told them that they were not from that land, but had traveled from a far country.

And they said unto him, From a very far country thy servants have come because of the name of the LORD.

Joshua 9:9

These men came with victuals, or food offerings, and requested a treaty with Joshua and Israel. Because the men from Gibeon told them they were not from the land, Joshua and the princes agreed to make a treaty with them. But Joshua and the men of Israel made a big mistake.

And the men took of their victuals, and ASKED NOT COUNSEL AT THE MOUTH OF THE LORD.

Joshua 9:14 (emphasis mine)

This is how the enemy often trips us up. Someone enters our life with a gift or something we desire, and we become so myopic and desirous of that gift that we fail to seek the opinion of the Lord.

And it came to pass at the end of three days after they had made a league with them, that they heard that they were their neighbors, and that they dwelt among them.

Joshua 9:16

Because of this ill-advised decision, Joshua and the princes were put to shame before the people.

And the children of Israel smote them not, because the princes of the congregation had sworn unto them by the LORD *God of Israel. And all the congregation murmured against the princes.*

Joshua 9:18

Many of us can look back on our lives and see how things could have been different if we had sought the will of God in a matter instead of forging our own way. Checking with God requires humility. The proud person will not pray prayers of inquiry because, in his heart, he believes he already knows what to do. As we humble ourselves before the Lord, checking with God will become an indemnity against failure, as well as a source of great joy!

The Pursuit of Happiness

The reason why many people today are operating in their own strength is because they are trying to find something called "happiness." Happiness is not of God; it is of the flesh. God's Word never admonishes us to be happy, instead, we are admonished to pursue contentment, peace and love. The enemy has blinded us to believe that we must find happiness in life rather than find the will of God for our lives. Many believers have determined that they will do God's will only after they find happiness. Because of this, the enemy will ensure that they never find happiness.

For where your treasure is, there will your heart be also.

Matthew 6:21

One day, I was speaking with a lady who was in search of the American dream. She was a Christian and assumed that her worldly ideology was of God. She said, "I want to make a better life for myself.

61

I want to live in a better community. I want my children to go to better schools. I want to have nice things." I commended her for her desire to get to a better state. However, the unfortunate thing was that God showed me that "a better state" had become her "god."

This world is not our home, yet many of us have clung to it as if there was no other life. In other words, we have abandoned the will of God to seek happiness. We are not to seek happiness in life, but rather we are to pursue the perfect will of God. Only then will we find happiness.

If ye then be risen with Christ, seek those things which are above, where Christ sitteth on the right hand of God. Set your affections on things above, and not on things on the earth. And when Christ, who is our life, shall appear, then shall ye also appear with him in glory.

Colossians 3:1-4

Finding happiness has become an American idol. Today, most people spend their lives looking for happiness!

For I came down from heaven, not to do mine own will, but the will of him that sent me.

John 6:38

Jesus didn't come into this world to be happy, He came to fulfill His destiny. Likewise, we did not come into this world to be happy. Happiness is the satanic substitute for walking in love, joy, peace and contentment.

Today, there are many studies on why people are so unhappy. People say things like, "I didn't marry the right person," "I need to get a degree," "I don't have enough money," "I want to be successful." The world is obsessed with happiness, and so are believers. Many believers are more in love with "church" as a concept than they are with Jesus as their Lord. In fact, I would go as far as to say that "church" is an idol for many believers.

If any man will come after me, let him deny himself, take up his cross and follow me.

Matthew 16:24

The message of Jesus is that we must give up our lives and die to ourselves. This intellectual generation has convinced the unsaved that we are "students" of God, but not "servants" of God. I was talking with a man in the hospital one day and he was sharing with me how miserable his life was. He hated his job, he hated his wife, and he hated himself. After listening to him for a while I said, "Sir, what you need is to allow Jesus Christ to come into your life."

He immediately calmed down and said, "I know, I know. My wife is always telling me that I need to go to church."

I said, "Sir, you don't need church. Church can do nothing for you. You need Jesus Christ."

The man replied, "I know I need to pray and read my Bible, but I work hard every day."

I said, "Sir, the Bible is no good until you have met the King; you need Jesus Christ."

We have turned meeting Jesus at the cross of surrender and servitude into an intellectual pursuit. We somehow want to believe that if we go to church and read our Bible, we can make our own lives better and somehow find happiness in our own strength.

Chapter 4

Intellectual False Adequacy

Modern ideology teaches us that our intellect is our ticket to success. Somehow we have bought into the idea that if we are smart, then we will be successful. We boast that our children are precocious, technologically savvy, and well-informed. The general idea is that smart equals successful. But many who have bought into this theory still find success eludes them. In fact, success in life is rarely predicated upon one's intellect alone.

There are a few in our society who, by intellect alone, are manifesting success; but there are a great many reasonable, intellectual, and analytical people who are not socially or financially successful. Relying on smarts for success can be a very false hope.

Some people study the Scriptures, not to know and fall in love with God, but rather to see how God's Word stacks up against their intellect. In effect, their relationship with God becomes less important than their reasoning about scriptural principles.

Today, one of the greatest signs of false adequacy is our reliance on our own intellect. We pride ourselves in being reasonable, rational, intellectual, and practical. We spend our time working to solve our problems while spending very little time praying. We are convinced that we must "figure out our problems" instead of relying on God for solutions. We wrestle with social problems—even in the church—with committees and conferences, but we fail to wrestle with these dilemmas in prayer.

> *Call unto me, and I will answer thee, and show thee great and mighty things, which thou knowest not.*
>
> Jeremiah 33:3

When someone has intellectual false adequacy, they are always striving to figure life out. They labor intellectually to advance themselves by reason. They see prayer as a religious act that only has symbolic significance. Jeremiah 33:3 is God's way of saying, "You don't know everything," or perhaps, "I am smarter than you!" There are things that are beyond our reasoning that we need God to reveal. To rely on our own intellect is to reject the need for God's voice in our lives.

Intellectual false adequacy keeps us from humbling ourselves and accepting the truth that God has all the answers. It causes us to feel like we have most, if not all, of the answers. If you are looking for a mate, there are people you don't know and things about those people you don't know. If you are looking for a job, there are jobs that you do not know of. If you are looking for a breakthrough, there are principles that you do not know. Only God can reveal these hidden things.

When someone deals with intellectual false adequacy, they will not pray because they don't believe in the power of God. Throughout the Scriptures, God declares many times, *"If you would hear my voice..."* (Psalm 95:7, Hebrews 3:7, Revelation 3:20). God disregards the intellect of man and summons him to obey His voice. There is nothing inherently wrong with intellect; intellect is of God. However, intellectual false adequacy is first and foremost a reliance upon our mind rather than reliance upon God. Intellectual false adequacy is a refusal to humble ourselves in order to hear from God.

The Root of Intellectual False Adequacy

Intellectual false adequacy begins with the notion that our mind is powerful. At some point, many people become impressed with their thoughts, believing they are superior to the thoughts of others. We forget that the simplicity of the men and women around us is not the measure by which we are judged. Our thoughts pale when compared to the mind of Christ.

One of the enemy's strongest deceptions is to get us to be impressed with our intellect. The intellect has actually become an idol or a god to many people. When we are overly impressed with our thoughts and the thoughts of others, the enemy can rule over our lives, bringing confusion. In our frustration, we try to think our way out, only to fall deeper into confusion. A contrite and surrendered heart is the only solution. We must bow before God and acknowledge that our intellect is useless without Him.

I consider myself an educated man. Education was for me (as is the case with so many) a source of personal pride. This pride is not easily distinguishable because the educated person often does not feel proud; he simply feels that others are ignorant. In his heart, he sees himself as separate or enlightened, while he sees others as backwards.

Education often makes us feel like we don't have to be humble. Humility becomes something that the uneducated man needs, not the educated man. Likewise, having money or status many times makes us feel that we are not required to be humble. Humility becomes something that is set aside for the poor. As a result, many saints in the Body of Christ are suffering from unchecked pride. They have identified something that they feel makes them better than others and have assumed that qualifies them for the office of "Judge of the World."

And the mean man shall be brought down, and the mighty man shall be humbled, and the eyes of the lofty shall be humbled: But the LORD of hosts shall be exalted.

Isaiah 5:15-16

Everyone wants a "claim to fame." In our pride, we are always in search of reasons why we are better than others. Employment, education, skills, intelligence, personal accomplishments, skin color, all are cited as evidence of superiority. However, we need to realize that all of these things are completely unimpressive to God. He is looking for a heart that is humble before Him—full of love for His people and obedient to His will.

Intellectual false adequacy is manifested in many ways. Suicide is an example of intellectual false adequacy because it represents man reaching the limits of his reasoning, and then responding in his own strength. Declared atheism is another example of intellectual false adequacy. Many have errantly placed their faith in science and have been deceived by the spirit of intellectual false adequacy. Science makes us feel intelligent, even powerful, but faith requires humility and acknowledgement of the greater power of God.

Those who deal with intellectual false adequacy are always trying to prove that they have a greater insight than others. Many have concluded that their intelligence sets them apart. Their goal is to prove to everyone around them how intellectually superior they are. If they are successful, the glory goes to them instead of God.

People who deal with intellectual false adequacy are obsessed with doing things their own way. Intellectual false adequacy is being impressed with our own thought life. It is also the inability to discern that our thoughts are not as impressive to God or to other people as they are to us. Intellectual false adequacy is the pride that says, "No one can think like me." Thinking that our thoughts are impressive, clever, insightful or analytical is often a trap of the enemy.

The Bible clearly teaches us that Satan is a deceiver (Revelation 20:1-3). One of his greatest deceptions is that of making someone believe that their intelligence makes them superior to others. With this misconception, the enemy is able to lead a person into a voluntary personal destruction. When we are impressed with our thought life, it produces pride—and pride is the enemy's playing field.

Intellectual pride is not always ostentatious and easily discerned by others; it is often kept as an inner pride that secretly hides within the heart. When we are impressed with our thoughts, God cannot reach us because the natural man cannot receive the things of God (1 Corinthians 2:14).

Intellectual false adequacy is often manifested as a refusal to be taught. People who practice intellectual false adequacy have a deep desire to know it all, but are unwilling to go through the humbling process of actually learning. They will feign knowledge rather than admit ignorance. Their mind has become their king and being perceived as the most knowledgeable is their crown.

Practitioners of intellectual false adequacy see a college degree as a sign of superiority and not as confirmation of a commitment to learning. Intellectual false adequacy causes them to want to feel like they figured things out for themselves. They will decline a very good suggestion or advice from someone just because it was not their own idea. To show that they are intellectually superior to others, they are constantly finding fault with other people's ideas, suggestions, and way of life.

People who deal with intellectual false adequacy rely on their analysis of everything. They believe that based solely on the strength of their reasoning, they can solve all their problems and live happily ever after. This negates the need for God in their life and consequently makes intelligence their god. This is a contradiction of faith. Faith is refusing to believe what you see and trusting God.

We walk by faith and not by sight.

2 Corinthians 5:7

Intellectual false adequacy is a tendency to believe only what can be perceived and deduced. Therefore, it is difficult for those who deal with this to walk by faith. Their analysis has more authority than the Word of God. They never allow God to speak to them through His Word; instead, they "analyze" the Bible.

A sick believer who is trapped by intellectual false adequacy spends his strength self-diagnosing and confirming his faith in pills and medical science instead of spending time in prayer. He prefers to believe that somehow his or his doctor's intellect will pull him through. Intellectual false adequacy is raising your children without introducing them to the fear of God, teaching them about science instead of faith and morals.

Many ministries today are operating on the strength of the pastor's intellect, which is far beneath the power of the Kingdom of God or the expectation of our heavenly Father. Yet, God's people have accepted it because they believe in the power of their intellect. If they want to see Kingdom results in their churches, their ministry must flow in the divine power that comes from the anointing of God, not from the reasoning of man's intellect.

Jesus was not an intellectual priest who went around arguing with the Pharisees and Sadducees. He rejected them and instead did miracles, signs and wonders like walking on water, turning water to wine, and healing miracles. These miracles were the result of the power of God operating in Jesus' life; they were not the product of human intellect.

Philosophical vs. Intellectual

Not all people are intelligent; some are merely philosophical. There is a big difference between being philosophical and being intellectual. Philosophy is simply a systematic way of thinking about things, while intellect is the ability to deduce, extract, analyze, and have effective insight about matters. Not everyone is intelligent, but anyone can be philosophical about anything just by having an opinion.

Some people who deal with intellectual false adequacy are naturally intelligent. Intelligence is a gift from God. Just as God endows men with the ability to sing or to paint, there is also the generational blessing of insight or intelligence. However, the gift of intelligence is not to be used to predicate superiority, but rather to minister to other people.

There are people who are gifted with insight about medicine or electronics or aeronautics or any other field, just as there are men who are gifted with athleticism or the ability to write or to draw. If your gifts were given to you by God, then we can safely conclude that God is not impressed that you have them. All endowments of God must be used in our rendering of service to mankind.

We err when we enjoy the talents of those whom God has gifted to sing or those whom God has gifted with athleticism, and then declare, "My intelligence is only for me." Every endowment from God is a talent and God will one day call for an account of our stewardship of it. Freely we receive, freely we must give (Matthew 10:8).

Intellectual Idolatry

And it came to pass on a certain day, as he was teaching, that there were Pharisees and doctors of the law sitting by, which were come out of every town of Galilee, and Judea and Jerusalem: and the power of the Lord was present to heal them.

Luke 5:17

If we scrutinize this scripture, one thing that conspicuously stands out is the description of the audience listening to Jesus on this certain day. The two groups of men who were listening to Jesus consisted of the Pharisees, who were the religious experts, and the doctors of the law, who were the scriptural experts.

This scripture suggests only that the power of the Lord was "present" to heal them. There is no indication that they "were healed," only that the potential for them to be healed was there. What is more curious is the fact that when healing is mentioned in Scripture, it is usually associated with the physically sick. But there is no suggestion in this verse that these men were physically sick. I would suggest that they were intellectually sick. It is a sickness to be so intellectually wired that you are unable to embrace the Son of God. Their intellect needed to be healed.

Since it also states that Jesus was teaching, this would imply that our minds can be healed under anointed teaching. These men could listen, scrutinize, and criticize Jesus' teaching, but because of their intellectual false adequacy, they could not come to Him and be saved. They needed God to heal their minds before they could be saved.

Intellectual false adequacy has made the mind an idol for many people—even for those within the church. The definition of an "idol" is anything or any person in your life that rivals your devotion to God. Intellectual false adequacy is idolatry, since it causes a person to worship his mind, intelligence, or ability to reason. We must come to the realization that intellect is inferior to revelation.

What takes us twenty years to understand in our intellect can take twenty seconds to realize with a revelation from God. In his intellect, it took Jacob fourteen years to acquire Rachel (Genesis 29), but with one revelation from God about the animals, Jacob transferred the wealth of Laban to himself in a very short period of time (Genesis 30:34-43).

Mental Wildernesses

And the LORD's anger was kindled against Israel, and he made them wander in the wilderness forty years, until all the generation, that had done evil in the sight of the LORD, was consumed.

Numbers 32:13

The children of Israel wandered in the wilderness for forty years because they would not humble themselves to accept God's will for their lives. God has shown me that many people today are wandering in a wilderness of intellectual false adequacy. This wilderness condition comes when an individual leans to his own understanding and then loses his grip on life (Proverbs 3:5).

Satan deceives us through our reliance upon our intellect. His strategy is to make us overly impressed with ineffective perspectives. Once we have embraced these faulty perspectives, our own thinking becomes a hindrance in our lives and we end up in a mental wilderness. His method for sowing deceptive thoughts into our minds may be through television, friends, family members, magazines, or a myriad of other sources.

Many believers today have been deceived by the enemy and have entered into a chronic state of broken relationship with the Lord. They go to church, but they cannot make heads or tails of their relationship with the Father. They don't know where God is, or where they are in relation to Him. Many do not know their way back into the will of God for their lives. Others are determined to live out their own will.

Intellectual false adequacy is evidenced when someone is presented with a choice in life and they become very strongly reliant upon their intellect and simultaneously resistant to hearing from God. When they experience failure in their lives, they humble themselves enough to casually acknowledge God, but once they see an opening, they bolt in rebellion again. This insistence upon relying on their mind severs their relationship with the Father and lands them in a perpetual intellectual wilderness.

Trust in the LORD with all thine heart: and lean not to thine own understanding. In all thy ways acknowledge Him and he shall direct thy paths.

Proverbs 3:5-6

People with intellectual false adequacy rely on their own understanding. Intellectual false adequacy is the misconception that we know the way and that others should follow our lead. We are always seeking to be the "chief." We don't want others to lead us, and we resent those who try to correct us.

One of the signs of intellectual false adequacy is unwillingness to learn something new. We deeply desire to prove our intelligency by "already knowing" things when they come up. People with intellectual false adequacy have big dreams that are nothing more than theory. Yet, they believe that somehow their theories will someday magically bring them success. They cling to their grandiose theories because they make them feel superior to others.

Intellectual false adequacy is shown when we try to teach someone who is more productive or knowledgable than we are. People who deal with intellectual false adequacy are self-proclaimed advisors; they know everything about everything. Intellectual false adequacy is being "textbook smart" about life.

Intellectual false adequacy is trying to fight a generational curse with our own reasoning, when it is obvious that we need the intervention of God. Intellectual false adequacy is blasphemously trying to explain away every instance of God's intervention in our lives in order to make ourselves look like we brought about the victory ourselves.

When questions arise, people who deal with intellectual false adequacy often dismiss an issue before they fully understand it. This is because they fear not having the answer, which would indicate that they are not intellectually superior. People who deal with intellectual false adequacy need to be right. They believe that they are not far away from having it all together in life, that there is just a little bit they haven't mastered and if they can just get that remaining knowledge, they will be able to excel at life. These people read many books looking for more knowledge about money, science, relationships, and even personal development. Yet, despite all their searching, their "Promised Land" remains always just beyond their grasp. For instance, it is not unusual to hear someone with intellectual false adequacy say, "I don't believe in tithing and giving a preacher my money." That person's confidence is in his reasoning and his ability to manage his own finances. Therefore, he rejects the Word of the Lord concerning tithing.

Intellectual false adequacy is not just a problem among the well-educated or the affluent. Many poor people depend on their intellect, and they are hindered because of it. For instance, one poor man was approached by an evangelist who offered to him salvation through Jesus Christ. The poor man understood what was being expressed to him, however, his reply was, "I have thought about all that religious stuff my entire life, sir, but it has not helped me get out of these bad living conditions."

This man is obviously impressed with his ability to think and to analyze his circumstances, but he is not yet convinced about his sins and his need to surrender and serve God. Once he comes to a conviction of his own inadequacy, he will be receptive to salvation and to prosperity. His faith in his intellect is his hindrance to receiving the free gift of salvation and all the other gifts of God.

Mental Torment

Thus saith the Lord, Cursed be the man that trusteth in man, and maketh flesh his arm, and whose hearth departeth from the Lord. For he shall be like the heath in the desert, and shall not see when good cometh; but shall inhabit the parched places in the wilderness, in a salt land and not inhabited.

Jeremiah 17:5-6

When someone deals with intellectual false adequacy, they have so many things going on in their head, it often stresses them out. This sets the stage for the "fear of the unknown." Many who trust in their intellect deal with the fear of the unknown. They fear they will fail at life because of something they were not able to handle or control.

Our minds are finite, but God is infinite. We know some things, but God knows all things. Many people falsely believe that they are somehow protected from catastrophe because they "stay on top of things." In this way, their intellect is their protector and their god. But those with intellectual false adequacy eventually grow weary of analysis and begin to fear what is coming next. The Bible says concerning the end times that,

Men's hearts will fail them for fear, and for looking after those things which are coming on the earth.

Luke 21:26

When we have not fully learned to trust God with our lives, we can only trust our intellect. But because our intellect is limited, we end up living in fear of what may happen next. We are constantly worrying about a gas shortage, stock market collapse, a destructive weather pattern, something happening to us or our family, or any other catastrophic event. Because we don't trust God with our lives, we feel we have to be on alert constantly and we do unnecessary things preparing for the "inevitable."

Those who adhere to intellectual false adequacy are often frustrated with the imperfections they see in themselves. They believe that if they somehow were perfect, they could manage their lives better. They are perfectionists. Their tendency is to try to fix their own lives, yet only God is truly wise and powerful enough to fix what is wrong with their life.

We can experience brokenness in our natural lives and our spiritual lives. When we find our lives broken, our tendency is to try to reason our way into health. We put much energy into figuring out how to make our lives better. We read self-help books to find answers.

While reading books is good, it is not good if it strengthens our faith in reason to the neglect of faith in God.

As a hospital chaplain working on a psychiatric unit, I have seen many believers come into the mental health ward. Many of these people were highly intelligent. When they were asked what caused their crash, they often said things like, "I was just having a lot of problems and I was doing all I could do to figure out how to fix it, but I ended up getting worse and worse."

Scripture says, *"Cursed be the man that trusteth in man"* (Jeremiah 17:5). We were not designed to figure out all our problems; we were designed to rely on God. Once we exhaust all our reasoning trying to figure it all out, fear sets in and then depression. When depression has run its full course, we find ourselves in a mental hospital.

Many patients in psychiatric units take medication for depression and say things like, "My life should be better. I have thought of everything I can think of, but my life still just keeps getting worse." This is based on the erroneous idea that our mind is our savior when in reality, our problems and imperfections are evidence of our inadequacy and our failure to rely on God.

When a child plays with a toy and the toy breaks, she will do everything she knows to do to fix it. Then after much effort, the only alternative is to take the toy to her father and ask him to fix it. When the father sees the toy, he knows exactly what has happened to it. Maybe the battery has fallen out, or maybe it is jammed.

We are like this child and our lives are like the toy. But all too often, instead of taking the toy to our Heavenly Father for repair, we continue to rely on our inadequate intellect to patch up the toy, rather than humble ourselves and ask our Father to fix it. Intellectual false adequacy is our effort to fix our lives in our own intellectual strength, rather than humbly asking God for His intervention.

Living Beneath Your Privilege

We live beneath our God-given privilege when we rely on our intellect because our intellect cannot deliver everything God has for us. God had many blessings for me that I could not receive because I was walking in the pride of my own mind. I knew of many things that I deeply desired, but I didn't know of many things God's desired to give me. If we continue to rely on our own intellect, we will always live beneath our privilege. We will never see the full will of God manifested in our lives.

Eye has not seen, ear has not heard, neither has it entered the heart of man, the things that God has in store for them that love Him.

1 Corinthians 2:9

"Coincidences"

Intellectual false adequacy is to assume, or prefer to believe, that blessings, opportunities, and favor are "coincidences" and not the direct divine intervention of God. When we claim coincidence, we give ourselves the credit and the glory for the blessings and favor God has brought to our lives. When God blesses, the man who has false adequacy claims the credit for the blessing, as if it was his intellect or wisdom that caused the miracle to happen. God is not glorified in the life of those who have intellectual false adequacy.

I will bless you, and you will glorify me.

Psalm 50:15

In this verse from Psalm 50, we get a glimpse of a mutually pleasing relationship between God and man. The saint is being blessed and God is being glorified. This two-way relationship is what the Father seeks. It is not a coincidence that the right person came along and helped you out when you were in need. That was God! It is not a coincidence that the car crash would have killed you if the brakes had not jammed. That was God! It is not a coincidence that when you were heartbroken and almost gave up, a peace came over you that kept you from committing suicide. That was God!

Our blessings do not come by coincidence. Every phase of our life is being shepherded by the Father. There are many things God has done for us that we have credited to ourselves, to others, or called a coincidence. This should not be.

One day, I was speaking with a pastor friend of mine and telling him how happy I was that God had blessed me with a job and a brand new car. I had been praying and believing God for financial breakthrough, employment, and a car. Despite bad credit, God favored me to purchase a brand new car with an excellent interest rate.

My friend listened to my praise report with indifference. Then he said, "But how did you get the car? Who financed it?"

I replied, "My job's credit union."

He replied in a very condescending voice, "Oh, you got that car through your job." He sought to omit the significance that God had favored me to get the car. I immediately felt that he was trying to say that the credit union deserved the praise. There are many people who have received blessings of all sorts and have given the glory to man. God blessed them, but they chose to give glory to their appearance, to their friends, to their luck—but never to God. God is not pleased with believers who pray to Him for a blessing and then when the blessing is received, give glory to everyone and anything else but Him.

Be not wise in thine own eyes; fear the LORD, depart from evil.

Proverbs 3:7

We must agree that the root of intellectual false adequacy is a natural arrogance that springs forth out of the human condition. The Apostle Paul identified and addressed this conceit in the Roman church when he wrote:

For I say, through the grace given unto me, to every man that is among you, not to think of himself more highly than he ought to think; but to think soberly, according as God hath dealt to every man the measure of faith.

Romans 12:3

Be of the same mind one toward another…Be not wise in your own conceits.

Romans 12:16

These two references from Romans chapter twelve give us a picture of the intellectual conceit that was resident in the church. Nothing is more destructive to our walk with the Lord than when the enemy makes us overly impressed with our intellect. Furthermore, nothing makes us more useless to God than when we spend our days operating in our limited intellectual strength. If we want to see the manifestation of the will of God in our lives, we must become far less impressed with our thoughts and opinions, and much more impressed with the power of God.

Chapter 5

Spiritual False Adequacy

While intellectual false adequacy is something we may observe in someone—saved and unsaved alike—spiritual false adequacy is something that occurs only in the believer. Many people today think it is sufficient to be religious or to just be "spiritual," but the work of God suffers as a result of our ineffective presentation of the gospel and the poor example we have set in this world. The Kingdom of God is not fully advancing as it should because the children of God are not properly relying on His strength. This world is waiting for the manifestation of the sons of God (Romans 8:19).

> *Not that we are sufficient of ourselves to think anything as of ourselves; but our sufficiency is of God. Who also hath made us able ministers of the new testament.*
>
> 2 Corinthians 3:5-6

Unfortunately, what we have been presenting to this world as the gospel is merely our own tawdry efforts at being religious. Until we realize that we are inadequate without God, we will not be able to win this world for Christ.

Let's take a look at the Apostle Paul's conversion. Keep in mind that before his conversion, Paul was known as Saul.

And Saul yet breathing out threatenings and slaughter against the disciples of the Lord, went unto the high priest, and desired of him letters to Damascus to the synagogues, that if he found any of this way, whether they were men or women, he might bring them bound unto Jerusalem.

Acts 9:1-2

Saul was a religious man. He had a certain understanding and appreciation for the things of God. Because of this, he was offended at those people who called themselves Christians. Saul set out in the name of God to persecute the Church that Jesus Christ had created. He believed he was doing this service for God, yet he was outside of God's will.

Saul represents the religious man who operates in his own strength, doing what he believes to be God's will. This is the picture of spiritual false adequacy. Many believers who boast that they are doing the service of God are really outside of the will of God. They are doing things for God based on their intellect or limited understanding of God's plan and purpose. In other words, they are doing the work of God without knowing or having a relationship with Him.

Spiritual false adequacy is doing the work of God without His guidance. Someone can preach the gospel or start a ministry and be outside of God's will, a Christian can marry another Christian person and be out of God's will, someone can even do good works and be out of God's will. These are all examples of spiritual false adequacy.

Spiritual/Religious Pride

Though I might also have confidence in the flesh. If any other man think that he hath whereof he might trust in the flesh, I more. Cir-

cumcised the eighth day, of the stock of Israel, of the tribe of Ben-jamin, an Hebrew of Hebrews, as touching the law, a Pharisee. Concerning zeal, persecuting the church; touching the righteousness which is in the law blameless. But what things were gained to me, those I counted loss for Christ.

Philippians 3:4-7

Spiritual false adequacy begins with personal spiritual or religious pride concerning our relationship with God. Paul, when speaking of his old life, stated that he had many spiritual trophies he could boast about. Saul's religious pride was derived from his Jewish background. Religious pride is prevalent in our churches today. Just as that pride led Saul to persecute the church, religious pride leads us to be insensitive to the will of God.

Spiritual pride is being impressed with our salvation, our spiritual gifts, our talents, our title, or our office. One may have religious pride about his relationship with God or his church title or who he is in Christ. Like Saul, this religious pride makes us insensitive to the will of God. Religious pride is a condition in which our relationship with God has induced internal assumptions of superiority.

Entitlement

As a result of religious pride and subsequent spiritual false adequacy, many spiritual people assume an attitude of entitlement. The word "entitlement" can have a positive meaning, referring to one's rights, privileges, or propriety, however, this entitlement can be false if it is not based on reality or truth. To be entitled is to have a right or a privilege to a particular benefit. Spiritual false adequacy is when we feel that God "owes us" because of the good deeds we have done, because we are spiritual, or because we have prayed.

When I was laboring under the duress of not having a car, I felt entitled to success because I was called to the ministry and gifted to teach the Bible. Since I felt entitled, I was not thankful for the blessings God had given me or for the people He sent into my life. This spirit of entitlement bred in me a personal arrogance and condescension toward others in the Body of Christ

I lived below my privileges in Christ because I felt that God was responsible for giving me success, as I defined it. I just sat around waiting for it to fall in my lap. I allowed myself to go without things I needed, thinking that God would somehow— one day—show others how great I am.

During this time, success evaded me on every hand. Finally, after twenty years of ministry, I had to accept the fact that I had not obtained success in my personal life or ministry. Although many people reason away their failures in life, I asked God why was it that others had obtained success, built ministries, bought houses, and raised families, while I was struggling in every way. I knew loved Him just as much as they did. God showed me that I had been stouthearted and walking in my own will, doing life in my own strength. It was a humbling awakening. God wanted to bless me, but He was waiting for me to turn to Him. I had to learn to do life His way, instead of my way!

God delights to bless His children by grace. However, God does not owe us anything. In fact, we cannot take credit for any good that is produced in us. All of our goodness and spiritual production is the result of the Lord's presence within us.

When God delivered me from spiritual false adequacy, He showed me that I had not been a good example for men to follow. Yet, because the Lord is within me, Jesus had been able to hide my weaknesses and faults and allow men to see Him instead of me. Sometimes we forget that it is Jesus who is doing the work within us.

God uses us despite ourselves, not because of ourselves. God, by His grace, empowers us to live a holy life, to operate in the gifts, to be endowed with the anointing, to preach the gospel, and to be a godly example. It is His grace at work—not us.

But ye shall receive power, after that the Holy Ghost is come upon you. And ye shall be witnesses unto me.

Acts 1:8

We cannot be effective witnesses without His divine assistance. Spiritual false adequacy is when we assume that we are effective because of our spirituality rather than because of the power of God's grace. Spiritual false adequacy is the false assumption that the Kingdom of God cannot function without us.

When we have spiritual false adequacy, we cannot take orders from people because we feel that we are better than they are because we are saved, because we are closer to God, or because we are holier than they are. Then we sit by and wait for God to show the world how anointed and blessed we are.

Spiritual false adequacy is when we feel that we don't need anyone to teach us anything because we believe that God will teach us what we need to know. It's feeling like people are obligated to assist us because of the godly way in which we live. Self-entitlement has made many ministers and pastors feel like they don't have to go to work. Some suffer needlessly while others abuse the people of God or the ministry. Many pastors feel that other people should pay their bills for them. This is all the result of the false sense of entitlement that spiritual false adequacy produces.

When we deal with spiritual false adequacy, we divide people into two groups: those who are better than us and those who are worse than us. In our mind, every person is either behind us or ahead of us, better off than us or worse off than us. We delight to write someone off as beneath us. As soon as we recognize a deficiency in another person, we declare them to be less than us. At the same time, we tend to be envious of those who have a little more than we have. We are always in competition with other believers, other churches, or other groups of people—just as Saul was in a competition with the Christians of his day.

And as he journeyed, he came near Damascus: and suddenly there shined round about him a light from heaven: and he fell to the earth, and heard a voice saying unto him, Saul, Saul, why persecutest thou me? And he said, Who art thou Lord? And the Lord said, I am Jesus whom thou persecutes.

Acts 9:3-5

Saul persecuted the Church to gain the recognition of the Pharisees and Sadducees. Spiritual false adequacy strives for titles while neglecting the matter of knowing God better. When we have spiritual false adequacy, we think we can do what we want to do because God is on our side. Many with spiritual false adequacy disobey the law. Something as simple as driving without a license can be a sign of spiritual false adequacy. Others may neglect to purchase insurance and assume God will keep them from having an accident or getting a ticket. It is not unusual for those who deal with spiritual false adequacy to lose their jobs for insubordination because they rebel against delegated authority on the premise that they serve a "higher authority"—God.

When we deal with spiritual false adequacy, we reject the person or thing we need the most because we refuse to accept that we are not self-sufficient. It is not unusual for a person who has spiritual false adequacy to feel that he doesn't need to listen to anyone because he or she listens to God. Spiritual false adequacy stems from a desire to show others that we are spiritually superior to them.

One of the signs of spiritual false adequacy is a refusal to accept help. This person may feel like refusing help is proof that they are relying on God. He may even refuse help under the guise of humility. However, if this rejection of help is related to proving to others that "God is on our side," it is spiritual false adequacy.

The person who has spiritual false adequacy may think within himself that he is on a higher level than other Christians because he walks closer to God. Spiritual false adequacy causes us to elevate ourselves above others in our thinking. It produces a works-righteousness or self-righteousness that the believer is often not even cognizant they have. Self-righteousness is, in its simplest form, the idea that we are worthy to be blessed. None of us are worthy to be blessed, but we are blessed because of Jesus. Works-righteousness is the idea that we are adequate on our own. But none of us are adequate without the power of God within us!

Knowledge

Now as touching things offered unto idols, we know that we all have knowledge. Knowledge puffeth up, but charity edifieth. And if any man think that he knoweth any thing, he knoweth nothing yet as he ought to know.

1 Corinthians 8:1-2

Knowledge is often the basis for spiritual false adequacy. Once a person begins to learn the Bible, get an understanding of spiritual things, and have a few experiences with the Lord, he may become impressed with his knowledge.

First Corinthians 8:1 says that, *"knowledge puffeth up."* This means there is a certain amount of pride that goes along with knowing the things of God. The Apostle Paul was endowed with the revelations of Jesus Christ. He was also enlightened with the mystery of the Church and the Word of God. The Apostle Paul says that because of the knowledge he carried, he was tempted by the sin of pride and self-exaltation.

And lest I should be exalted above measure through the abundance of the revelations, there was given to me a thorn in the flesh, the messenger of Satan to buffet me, lest I should be exalted above measure.

2 Corinthians 12:7

Believers whom God allows to see into the spirit realm, those to whom the Holy Spirit imparts the spirit of prophecy, those who develop a certain amount of knowledge from the study of the Scripture, and those who have special divine experiences, all have one thing in common—special knowledge. Since knowledge has the potential to produce pride, these believers may begin to view this special knowledge as evidence that God sees them as better than the common believer. Once this happens, this knowledge has become the foundation for spiritual false adequacy.

Knowledge has spoiled many dedicated believers. Because they have spiritual knowledge, they have stopped seeking God and have begun operating in their own spiritual strength. They fail to understand that knowledge is a gift from God that He expects them to steward.

In this modern era, knowledge about God has replaced having a relationship with God. The fallacy is in thinking that because we know some things about God, God should be impressed with us and bless us. This generation needs to renounce the pursuit of spiritual knowledge and begin to covet a relationship with God. There are many in our churches today who have read hundreds of books about God, yet have never heard a word from God. We are not great because we have knowledge, just as a cup is not great because it holds an expensive beverage. Spiritual knowledge is the property of God. It is given to us on assignment as a tool for our work. It is not the evidence of our greatness; it is the evidence of His greatness.

As a pastor and teacher of the Word, God graced me to have revelation knowledge of the Bible. Because of this knowledge, I began to take on the mentality that I was better than other pastors and teachers. One day, God spoke to me and said, "That is My Word you are carrying and not your own." When we exalt ourselves because of our knowledge, we disrespect God's glory. We are to use the knowledge God has given us to bring glory to God, not exalt ourselves.

But we have this treasure in earthen vessels, that the excellency of the power may be of God, and not of us.

2 Corinthians 4:7

If a man thinks he is something when he is nothing he deceiveth himself.

Galatians 6:3

Some people believe that they are qualified to do the work of God because they have knowledge. They falsely believe that a seminary degree qualifies them to stand on God's platform and speak for God. They rely on their weak spiritual intellect that is tainted with thoughts of the flesh and of the devil. When they do this, they cause embarrassment and damage to the people of God and to the Kingdom of God.

Spiritual false adequacy creates formulas for God. What we call doctrine actually trivializes God and limits His power in our lives.

When we do not seek God, we continually share our paltry knowledge of God with other people. We become insistently dogmatic about the things of God because we are relying on our intellect and not fresh revelation from God.

Spiritual false adequacy causes the grace of God to no longer fall upon our ministry because we are preaching by intellect, instead of by the power of the Spirit of God. Spiritual false adequacy is when we believe that our perspective on God is all there is to know about Him. We become resistant to new perspectives of God. When we deal with spiritual false adequacy, we think our spiritual calling is to be a critic. In other words, we believe God has called us to criticize other ministers and ministries.

Promotion/Elevation

For promotion cometh neither from the east, nor from the west, nor from the south. But God is the judge: he putteth down one and setteth up another.

Psalm 75:6-7

The LORD maketh poor, and maketh rich: he bringeth low, and lifteth up. He raiseth up the poor out of the dust, and lifteth up the beggar from the dunghill, to set them among princes, and to make them inherit the throne of glory: for the pillars of the earth are the LORD's, and he hath set the world upon them.

1 Samuel 2:7-8

Spiritual false adequacy is being impressed with ourselves and the anointing we carry. We have seen God work through us and now we are impressed—not impressed with God; impressed with ourselves.

Our desire is for the world to see that we have the "anointing." We are impressed with our spiritual production. We are impressed with our spiritual gifts. Because we recognize the virtue in ourselves, we have declared our worthiness for elevation. Instead of being humble and staying at the feet of Jesus, we are daily seeking our own personal promotion.

Many are trying to use the gift that God has given them to exalt themselves. They are constantly seeking a stage on which to speak or preach. But I remind you that God has to exalt you; your gift cannot exalt you and you cannot promote yourself. There are many men and women of God who are waiting on promotion from the Lord. However, if God does not yet see them as ready to be promoted, they are not ready for promotion, no matter how impressed they may be with themselves. When they get ahead of God and try to promote themselves, such self-promotion is pride.

Spiritual false adequacy is having an agenda to promote and glorify oneself. Many are not aware of this sin, because they judge themselves by their good intentions. They think, *I want to preach and do work for God.* The reasoning is, since they want to do it for God, there can be no fault in it. Thus they remain blinded to their own glory-seeking. When every choice and action is motivated by the effort to put ourselves into the spotlight, we become insensitive to the reality that none of us deserve the glory for our ministries. We must remember that Jesus Christ is the only One the Father is trying to glorify.

When we deal with spiritual false adequacy, we find a way to attribute every breakthrough that happens in our life or in the lives of people we influence to ourselves. It is not uncommon for us to say things like, "God brought you out because I prayed for you!" or "Because you are under my ministry, you are being blessed." These statements are errant because they neglect to give God the glory. We are not great—He is great!

Consider this story. Three ministers were driving home one day from a certain religious service. During the service, one man had come down and given his life to the Lord. As these men drove, they were all very proud of the fact that someone had gotten saved. One of the ministers said to the other two, "Why do you all think the man got saved tonight?"

Another minister replied, "Oh, that is obvious. He got saved because of the powerful prayers I prayed during the service."

The next minister interjected, "No sir, this man got saved because when I talked during the service, I always give sound doctrine. It was the correct doctrine that convinced him that he needed Jesus."

The third minister then said, "Not true sir, this man was saved because of the anointing that is on my life. I sang under the anointing and it affected the man's decision."

All three ministers felt that it was their personal spiritual adequacy that rendered the results. They were all giving themselves the glory for what God had done.

So then neither he who plants is anything, nor he who waters, but God who gives the increase.

1 Corinthians 3:7

Anything good that comes out of our ministry is the result of the presence of Jesus Christ within us and the power of God backing us. God does the work. We are simply the vessels He works through. We have no boast in this matter. We should be grateful that despite all our imperfections, God still chooses to use us.

When we have spiritual false adequacy, we are very proud of our church, group, or religious affiliation. Our goal becomes making ourselves and our church look good. This makes us insensitive to our God-given assignment in the Body of Christ. Today, many believers have made promoting their church the goal of their faith. They fail to understand that their passion for their church is nothing more than an extension of their desire to promote themselves.

When a believer has fallen in love with Jesus Christ and Him only, their devotion is not to their church, but to the Lord and His Kingdom. Church is not the goal of the Christian life. Exalting Jesus Christ is the goal of the Christian life. Yet many have invested their lives into promoting the pastor and church facilities.

Spiritual false adequacy is being more impressed with attendance numbers, offerings, and church facilities than we are with having a relationship with God. Our hope should be in Christ and Him alone. Whether we are in a church of two or three, or in a church of thousands, we should have the same passion. Jesus Christ is building "His Church," not "our church."

In our society today, many churches need to merge. They are both serving and praying to the same God, yet they are too proud to come together under one rooftop. The pastors desire to prove their own spiritual adequacy. Spiritual false adequacy is when a minister stays in his own strength rather than humbling himself and seeking God's will for his ministry. Spiritual false adequacy is being too proud to admit we have failed at ministry or at life.

Refusal to listen to or depend on others is one of the greatest evidences of spiritual false adequacy. One young believer, full of spiritual false adequacy, was struggling with her life. She was born again and boasted of her relationship with God. She was very proud of her kinship to God. She was an ambitious young minister and wanted the things of God in her life, but she wanted to have them her own way. She was very resistant to other believers speaking into her life. When she was advised by other saints, she would often say, "If God wants me to know that, He will tell me." In her pride, she wanted to bypass her need for the rest of the Body of Christ. Her biggest struggles stemmed from her pride and her inner desire to be promoted. Yet her inadequacy was reflected in every area of her life.

Lordship

And he fell to the earth, and heard a voice saying to him, Saul, Saul, why persecutes thou me? And he said, Who art thou, Lord? And the Lord said, I am Jesus whom thou persecutest: it is hard for thee to kick against the pricks. And he trembling and astonished said, Lord, what wilt thou have me to do? And the Lord said unto him, Arise, and go into the city, and it shall be told thee what thou must do.

Acts 9:4-6

Saul of Tarsus was the poster child for spiritual false adequacy. When we are full of spiritual false adequacy, we behave just like Saul. Saul was in it for his own glory. Saul was operating on his own personal ideas about God, instead of on a revelation from God. Being a Pharisee made him feel superior to others and entitled to persecute their faith. His knowledge of the things of God informed him that he was to be preferred before others; therefore, he sought promotion from the high priest and the Sanhedrin.

However, Saul was delivered from his spiritual false adequacy as he fell to the ground on the road to Damascus. This is the key to overcoming spiritual false adequacy. When Saul fell to the ground, it represented a humbling of himself. When Saul humbled himself, he got a special revelation. He received the revelation that "Jesus is Lord."

When we deal with spiritual false adequacy, the root of our problem is that we do not have a full understanding of the lordship of Jesus Christ. We may know him as Savior, but his lordship is far from us. This does not mean that we are not doing many things in the Lord's name. Saul thought that his actions were endorsed by God. However, we know they were not.

Those who deal with spiritual false adequacy are doing many things in the name of the Lord Jesus, but the will of the Father they have not sought to know.

Not everyone that saith unto me, Lord, Lord, shall enter into the kingdom of heaven; but he that doeth the will of my Father which is in heaven. Many will say to me in that day, Lord, Lord, have we not prophesied in thy name? and in thy name have cast out devils? And in thy name done many wonderful works? And then will I profess unto them, I never knew you, depart from me, ye that work iniquity.
Matthew 7:21-23

Just because we call Jesus Lord or do things in the name of Jesus, does not mean we are in submission to the Father. Religious activity does not mean that we know the Lord. Only those who have made a deliberate decision to search out the will of God and obey it have come to know Jesus as Lord. In this text concerning Saul's conversion on the Damascus road, the man we knew as Saul, who was articulate to speak with the high priest concerning religious matters, was changed. He was humbled in his inner man. He was only able to ask two questions: "Who art thou Lord?" and "Lord, what wilt thou have me to do?" Notice that the word "Lord" is present in both statements. Saul had been broken. His religious energy had been dispensed for obedience. He wanted to know and do God's will, not his own will.

When he began his journey, Saul was a man who was religious, operating in his own religious strength. But on the road to Damascus, he encountered the Lord Jesus. There on the road, the man Saul died and a new man, Paul, arose. The Lord then instructed Paul to go into the city and it would be told him what he must do. Paul obediently did what the Lord told him to do. He was no longer operating in his own religious energy; he was operating by the mandate of the Lord Jesus.

This man, Paul, who had letters from the high priest to arrest and enslave Christians, was now submitting himself to Ananias for prayer (Acts 9:17). Likewise, when we fully and unconditionally submit to the lordship of Jesus Christ, the bondage of spiritual false adequacy will be broken. Then, the way we view the work of God, who we are willing to submit ourselves to, and how we go about our ministry, will all drastically change for the better.

Chapter 6

Self-Life

The word "self" refers to the essence of our being; it is the constitution of the person we have become. There are many modern terms that reference the self: self-seeking, self-willed, self-exaltation, self-help, self-analysis, self-serving, self-expression, self-conscious, and many others. When "self-life" is mentioned in this chapter, I am speaking of a life that is unyielded to God.

Self-life is the opposite of living the God-centered life. Self-life can be generally defined as living for yourself, or attending to the things of the flesh and of this world. More specifically, the self-life is allowing the nature of the flesh to rule instead of the Spirit of God. In the self-life, we are our own god and the things that we desire are our idols. The self-life is to believe in ourselves instead of believing wholly in the power of God. If the self is not put down, we will not follow Jesus.

If any man would come after me, let him deny himself.
Matthew 16:24

The self-life may be manifested in different ways in different individuals. "Self" is the idol in many people's closets. Some evidences of the self-life are a spirit of pride, love of praise, worldliness, being self-willed, dishonest, or religious. These are just a few of the indicators that a person is living for self. Jesus was referencing the self-life when He said, *"Whosoever will save his life shall lose it,"* (Matthew 16:25).

God makes us all individually. There is no "cookie cutter" in God's production. Every person has a unique personality. Sigmund Freud called it the "id" of our personality; we may refer to it as the "me," "myself," or the "I" of life. Whatever we call it, without submission to Christ, we live for ourselves.

Self-life refers not only to the thoughts and ideas of a person, but to their very constitution. A person's constitution has to do with who they are, what they stand for, and how they are. Your constitution is the deepest, most established part of you. For Jesus to be Lord over your life, it will not suffice for you just to seek to accept His precepts and ideas in your mind intellectually. For Jesus to be Lord of your life, your very constitution must be broken and changed. A broken constitution is all that God will accept from us.

Years ago as God started dealing with me, He was shaping me into the man He called me to be. One day, God gave me a spiritual vision. In this vision I saw a thick piece of wood that was planted deep into the ground. I intuitively knew that the piece of wood represented me and my constitution as a person. In the vision, I saw that same piece of wood suddenly broken. It still stood in the same place, but it was severely cracked. The crack could be clearly seen. I knew intuitively that God was showing me that He was breaking my constitution that had been long established.

After that vision, I became much more amenable to becoming the man God was calling me to be. When Saul met Jesus on the Damascus Road, his constitution was broken and he replied, "What will you have me to do, Lord" (Acts 9:1-6). Today, men feign obedience, but their constitution remains intact. These believers speak of God, but refuse to submit to His plans, purposes, and direction.

God cannot pour into pitchers that are already full. You must pour out yourself if you want God to fill you. Often when a believer has had a lot of humbling experiences in her life, it's because God is trying to break her self-life. When our self-life is strong, God has to allow our failures to humble us. But we should remember, it is possible to be humbled by our circumstances while remaining unbroken internally.

> *Whosoever will save his life shall lose it.*
>
> Matthew 16:25

We often think of this text as applying to the unbeliever. However, I have often found that after we are born again, we try to take our lives back from God in a foolish quest to live life by our own standards. This represents an unbroken constitution. But thanks be to God that He knows how to break our constitutions. God is dealing with His children. Moses was dealt with in the desert. Joseph was dealt with in prison. David was dealt with in the cave at Adullam. Paul was dealt with in Arabia. Israel was dealt with in the wilderness. Now God is dealing with us!

We Must Die to Ourselves

In order for a believer to live under the lordship of Christ, he must die to himself. The Bible speaks of three types of dying: dying to self, dying to sin, and dying to this world. Our identity with Christ is identity with His death.

> *What shall we say then? Shall we continue to sin, that grace may abound? God forbid. How shall we, that are dead to sin, live any longer therein? Know ye not, that so many of us as were baptized into Jesus Christ were baptized into his death?*
>
> Romans 6:1-3

Knowing this, that our old man is crucified with him, that the body of sin might be destroyed, that henceforth, we should not serve sin.

Romans 6:6

When Jesus went to the Cross, He slew our old nature so that it would be easy for us to mortify it. Jesus slew it and broke its power, but the rest is left up to us.

And they that are Christ's have crucified the flesh with the affections and lusts.

Galatians 5:24

Sin does not rule over those who have fully yielded themselves to Jesus Christ. We are not just to identify with Jesus, but we are to identify with His death on the Cross.

We are buried with him by baptism into death.

Romans 6:4

When we get water baptized in the church, we are identifying ourselves with Jesus' death. Since Jesus died *for* this world, we are to die *to* this world. The more we identify with His death, the more He reigns over our lives. This is what the Apostle Paul meant when he wrote:

I am crucified with Christ, nevertheless I live.

Galatians 2:20

This generation has not known lordship because it has not known the death of self.

And that he died for all, that they which live should not henceforth live unto themselves, but unto him which died for them, and rose again.

2 Corinthians 5:15

This scripture speaks of "not living for ourselves." Many believers today speak of Christ, yet they live for themselves. Their lives are lived in a selfish, self-serving manner. Until believers die to themselves, they cannot demonstrate to this world sufficient light to cause unbelievers to see their need for the Lord.

Always bearing about in the body the dying of the Lord Jesus, that the life also of Jesus might be made manifest in our body. For we which live are always delivered unto death for Jesus' sake, that the life also of Jesus might be made manifest in our mortal flesh. So then death worketh in us, but life in you.

2 Corinthians 4:10-12

We must die to this world and the things of this world. When those who are saved are still alive to this world, the unsaved man sees no distinction between him and the believer. He is greedy and so is the believer. He is living a life of sin and so is the believer. He lives to promote himself and so does the believer. There is absolutely no difference.

Many believers erroneously believe that they are here on earth to promote themselves and that it is God's job to assist them. This could not be further from the truth. Every believer should be busy dying to himself, to this world and to the things of this world. Too many modern-day Christians simply love this world. We must die to our self-life, to sin, and to this world.

Love not the world, neither the things that are in the world. If any man love the world, the love of the Father is not in him. For all that is in the world, the lust of the flesh, and the lust of the eyes, and the pride of life, is not of the Father, but is of the world.

1 John 2:15-16

If ye then be risen with Christ, seek those things which are above, where Christ sitteth on the right hand of God. Set your affections on things above, and not on things on the earth. For ye are dead, and your life is hid with Christ in God. When Christ, who is our life, shall appear, then shall ye also appear with him in glory.

Colossians 3:1-4

This scripture from Colossians 3 is simply saying, "You are dead." This is the way God sees us with respect to this world. Our life was in Christ when He went to the Cross and now His reality is our reality. Naturally speaking, on the Cross, Jesus was at one point physically dead. But today, Jesus Christ is alive forevermore. If you do not die to who you used to be, you will never become who God called you to be.

If any man will come after me, let him deny himself, and take up his cross daily, and follow me.

Luke 9:23

Our commitment to self-life is most evident in how we struggle with giving to the Lord and to others. Money represents our life, our hopes, and our dreams. It represents our ambitions and our love for this present world. When we give our money to the Lord, we establish our submission to Him, and we show this world we are yielded to God and to the things of God. But if our self-life is ruling, then giving to God will be avoided.

Many Christians today have a sort of twisted theology that says, "I live for my own self and I will employ God to assist me." It is man's job to glorify the Father, not the Father's job to glorify man. We may ask why the modern-day church has been less effective in influencing this world with the gospel. The answer is simple. Without dying, our influence will remain small. But if we die, we will, like Jesus, bring many souls to God's kingdom.

> *Verily, verily, I say unto you, except a corn of wheat fall into the ground and die, it abideth alone: but if it die, it bringeth forth much fruit.*
>
> John 12:24

Mephibosheth: Living Beneath Your Privileges

> *And the king said unto him, Where is he? And Ziba said unto the king, Behold, he is in the house of Machir, the son of Ammiel, in Lodebar.*
>
> 2 Samuel 9:4

After David became king of Israel, he reflected back on those who supported him during the times when he was a nothing. David remembered the kindness of his friend Jonathan and sought to show kindness to the descendents of Jonathan and Saul. Although many of the descendents of both Saul and Jonathan were dead, there was a servant in David's house who knew that there was a son of Jonathan who was still alive. His name was Mephibosheth. Since he was the grandson of King Saul, he should have been living like a king, but instead he was living beneath his privilege in a place called Lodebar. I actually like to break the word "Lodebar" down this way—Below-the–Bar.

Mephibosheth is a reminder to us that when we allow our self-life to rule, we will live below God's privilege for our lives. It is God's will to give us more, but we are unable to receive it because of our mindset. Perhaps Mephibosheth felt that his crippled feet disqualified him from claiming nobility.

We live beneath our privilege when we believe that the deficit and lack we are experiencing in life is God's will for us. We live beneath our privilege when we accept a standard of living that is less than what has been endowed to us by God. We live beneath our privilege when we agree to live on welfare, disability, unemployment, or food stamps instead of claiming God's inheritance for our lives. Mephibosheth was the son of a king, but he was living as a beggar. We, too, are the sons and daughters of a King. Does our lifestyle reflect that fact?

The enemy works to keep us ignorant of the fact that we are the sons and daughters of God (1 John 3:2). One of the consequences of false adequacy is living beneath our privilege. When we deal with false adequacy, what we expect in life is based on what we believe we are able to acquire ourselves. With regards to Mephibosheth, one would assume that being crippled meant that he would have easily recognized his limitations and his need for assistance. Unfortunately, more often than not, those who have the greatest deficits in life are the ones who are full of false adequacy.

Mephibosheth was living in Lodebar because of false adequacy. However, David fetched Mephibosheth and brought him to the king's table. David restored the inheritance of Jonathan to Mephibosheth and gave him both an wealth and servants (2 Samuel 9:5-10).

Mephibosheth was humble enough to receive what David was offering, but too often the pride of false adequacy will cause people to reject the blessings of the Lord. False adequacy makes us want to earn our blessings instead of being humble enough to receive them by faith. Mephibosheth went from being "a dead dog" in his own eyes, to sitting among the king's sons. We, too, can graduate from our low estate if we accept the fact that the way up is actually down.

There is another assault that comes upon the believer's mind and we call it complacency. Complacency is defined as a feeling of contentment or self-satisfaction associated with being unaware or un-informed of pending danger; a smug or uncritical satisfaction with oneself or one's accomplishments; to compromise with yourself or with the enemy concerning your potential; or to agree to accept less. Living beneath our privilege and living in complacency are very similar. However, they differ in this way. Living beneath our privilege is to not be aware of what is rightfully ours. Complacency is knowing what is ours but being unwilling to do what is necessary to secure it.

There are many complacent believers in the kingdom. There is physical laziness and there is mental laziness. Over the years, God has shown me that the enemy has sown tares of complacency in my mind so I would not go after the things that I deserve as a child of God. Because I was not willing to fight for or work for my inheritance, I became a victim of complacency. One of the principles we learn from Joshua and the Israelites is that even though God had given them the Promised Land, they had to possess it themselves.

And there remained among the children of Israel seven tribes, which had not yet received their inheritance. And Joshua said unto the children of Israel, How long are ye slack to go to possess the land, which the LORD God of your fathers hath given you.

Joshua 18:2-3

There are many things God has endowed to us, but our enemy will not allow it to be brought to us on a silver platter. We must fight for what is rightfully ours. God was with Israel when they entered the Promised Land. They did not suffer from a lack of God's support. It was, instead, their reluctance to fight that kept them outside of the blessings of their inheritance.

Complacency says, "I don't want to fight for it, and God won't make it easy for me, so I might as well let it go." Complacency is an enemy of the believer. Rise up and slay complacency! And then let us get back into the fight to receive all that God has for us.

The Life of Jacob

Jacob's life is an example of God crucifying the self-life. The word "Jacob" means deceiver or supplanter, and such was true of the man from his birth. Jacob inherited his self-life from his mother Rebekah. She was a crafty woman and taught Jacob to be the same way. It was Rebekah who provided Jacob leadership as they deceived Isaac and stole the blessing away from Esau (Genesis 27). This was probably how she handled Isaac over the years.

Throughout the life story of Jacob, we find him tricking and deceiving. Like many people today, Jacob was spiritual, but had many character defects. He was spiritual enough to value the birthright and his father's blessing, but the means by which he went about securing these things was dubious, at best. This is the picture of an individual whose self is strong. He acknowledges God in some ways, yet his life is unyielded to God in other ways.

When someone has a strong self-life, they may be a very spiritual person, but they have not yet learned to submit to the ways and means of the Lord. With the help of Rebekah, Jacob's usurped the blessing from his brother Esau by deceiving his father, Isaac. However, for Jacob, only half the battle was won. He had obtained a provisional right to the blessing, but now he had to turn to God to actually receive it. (Genesis 28:1-4, 16-22) At Bethel, Jacob has his first encounter with God. Bethel is the place of conversion for Jacob.

In this spiritual experience, God introduced Jacob to the new life. It is at Bethel that Jacob became a spiritual man. He was still Jacob. He still had the character of a supplanter and a trickster, but he began learning and growing in the things of God. At Bethel, he had his first vision and it made a tremendous impression on his life. God's goal was to root out all the self-life from Jacob. Jacob was crafty, manipulative, tricky, and deceptive. This was his natural self. Therefore, God endeavored to change Jacob by sending him to someone who had the same type of crafty ways. God guided Jacob to Laban, who was a manipulator and a thief. For the next twenty years, Jacob had to deal with the craftiness of Laban. Jacob knew "the game," but Laban invented "the game."

For more than fourteen years, Laban tricked Jacob out of his money and his wife. During this time, Jacob steadily lost confidence in himself. By Genesis 30:26, Jacob was maturing and finally decided to confront his uncle's treachery. Jacob realized that Laban meant him no good. He purposed in his heart to leave Laban. Jacob made a demand for his wives and his children.

Laban, however, was just as crafty as ever. He realized that God had blessed his home because of Jacob and he determined to keep Jacob in his employ. Just as Jacob had stolen the blessing from Esau, so Laban was stealing the blessing from Jacob. Laban set out to make a deal with Jacob to pay him wages and keep him tied to himself. But Jacob was not to be denied. During the years Jacob had labored for Laban, he had learned to hear from God. His self-life was dying and he was learning to do things God's way. He had come to realize that the prosperity on Laban's life rightfully belonged to him. After receiving a revelation from God, Jacob made a business deal with Laban over the cattle. God had given Jacob revelation on how to transfer the wealth of Laban to himself.

Jacob learned to recognize that God was the source of his blessings, not the ingenuity of his flesh (Genesis 30:27-31). Jacob left Laban victorious, having obtained both his wives and his wealth. After dealing with Laban, Jacob had to return home and face his greatest fear—his brother Esau. This is the work of the Lord in our lives.

God does not intend that we live our lives running from that thing that makes us fearful. We must only fear God. Jacob set out to face his brother Esau. On his way there, the angel of the Lord met him. As God continued to deal with Jacob, Jacob continued to lose confidence in his self-life and his spiritual man grew stronger. Jacob found out that his brother Esau was coming to meet him with four hundred men (Genesis 32:6). Jacob feared for the worst and was faced with a decision. Would he revert to depending on his craftiness in this situation or would he rely on the power of God?

In Genesis 32:7, Jacob sets his people in array. This was his craftiness at work. But in Genesis 32:8-12, he prayed and asked God for deliverance. This was his spiritual man at work. Jacob was still a trickster, but he was also a man who was learning to yield to God.

Jacob sent his people on ahead and was left alone where he wrestled with an angel all night long. This wrestling is significant because it is during that night that God broke Jacob's self-life. Jacob took a hold of Jesus Christ that night in the form of an angel, and would not let Him go. This wrestling match brought about a new spiritual reality for Jacob. He would no longer be called Jacob; God gave him a new identity and the name "Israel." The name Jacob means trickster or supplanter, but the name Israel means "a prince with God." Jacob's transformation was complete. He had become a new man. The old nature had been conquered and subdued. Jacob had become a new creature.

The Jacob we once knew was now Israel. The Trickster had become the Prince. No longer would Jacob be ruled by his self-life; now he would be ruled by the Spirit of God. This is indicative of our new life in Christ. We are changed internally, but that change then has to work itself outward. Jacob's thigh was broken while wrestling with God and so was his self. He had been dealt with by God. From that day forward, he walked with a limp, which was evidence of his brokenness.

When God breaks false adequacy from our lives, the "limp" we bear is humility and sensitivity to God's will. Other believers still clinging to their own strength have not been broken. But those who have come to realize that they are inadequate without God rejoice to "limp" for Him. As Jacob's life progresses, he is referred to mostly by his new name, Israel. This is his spiritual name and the name that God references. God has ways of causing us to lose confidence in our flesh. Until we have the character God is looking for, He leaves us to the world. God will allow the world's system to deal with us until we have emptied ourselves.

Joseph

By the thirty-seventh chapter of Genesis, we find that Israel has twelve sons, but he has a special love for his son Joseph. Joseph becomes the central figure of the text at this point. And as with all generational cycles, Joseph is susceptible to some of the same weaknesses as his father Jacob.

Joseph is a very spiritual young man. A casual reading of Joseph's life story implies that he is the son who is most loyal to his father. Israel loves Joseph because he is his youngest son, probably born to him in his old age (Genesis 37:3).

While Israel is impressed with Joseph, God has some lessons that He needs to teach him. Many of us got saved and maybe at some point in our lives, felt we basically had it all together. We thought that since we were not like the heathens of this world, we were qualified to sit on the throne. However, as Joseph would come to learn, many of God's children are not nearly as prepared for the will of God as they may think they are.

Joseph operated in his spiritual gift at a young age. He was a gifted seer and had the specialty of interpreting dreams. He was not shy, bashful, or humble about his gifting or his dreams. In fact, he wanted everyone to check out his dreams (Genesis 37:6).

Joseph dreamed a dream about sheep. This dream was not difficult to interpret. He told his brothers that the primary point of the dream was that their sheep were bowing down to his sheep. Joseph's brothers said to him, *"Shall thou indeed reign over us"* (Genesis 37:8). Joseph's dream would prove accurate; however, he had no idea of the transformation that must take place in him before his dream could be realized. God gives us the spirit of prophecy to encourage us down the long road we have to journey.

Joseph eventually had another dream. This next dream was about the sun, moon, and the stars. The gist of this dream was that the sun, the moon, and eleven stars all bowed down and worshipped Joseph (Genesis 37:10). There were eleven stars in the dream and Joseph had eleven brothers. The sun would then represent Israel, Joseph's father, and the moon would represent Joseph's mother. It seemed that none of the family was confused about the interpretation of this dream either. Joseph's father said to him, *"Shall I and thy mother and thy brethren indeed come to bow down ourselves to thee"* (Genesis 37:10).

Joseph probably thought that this dream would just happen overnight. But if you have been walking with God for any period of time, you probably have learned that God will show you where you are going to encourage you, but He does not always tell you everything you will have to go through before you get there. Joseph had the gift, but he did not yet have the character to be used by God. Having a gift without godly character will bring shame to you, and to God. Therefore, when you are gifted, you must submit to God so He can develop His character in you.

Joseph was spiritual, but he was also proud. God had to work on him to break the false adequacy off of his life. God had to set him free from pride so that he could become useful to Him. Often, the more anointed you are, the greater the trial. Joseph was gifted—but still not trained.

Joseph's brothers were jealous of him and they conspired to sell him into slavery (Genesis 37:18-27). A band of Ishmaelites purchased Joseph and took him down to Egypt where he was sold to a man named Potiphar (Genesis 37:36). Once he was a slave in Egypt, Joseph began his training for reigning. This training would work in him the character of God.

Through all that Joseph experienced, we are reminded that the Lord was with him (Genesis 39:2). In Potiphar's house, Joseph was tested. There are two tests that every believer must pass before they are qualified for elevation. One is the test of faithfulness with money. The other is mastery of the flesh. In Potiphar's house, Joseph was tested with both.

God elevated Joseph and he became the overseer of Potiphar's house. Joseph was placed in control of all of Potiphar's material possessions. God was watching Joseph and found him faithful in finances, as is witnessed by the fact that God blessed Potiphar's house for Joseph's sake (Genesis 39:5-6). Joseph's next test was that of the flesh. Potiphar's wife set her eyes on Joseph to sleep with him. Again, Joseph passed his test, refusing to sleep with his master's wife (Genesis 39:7-19).

But after Joseph did the right thing, he was falsely accused and sentenced to prison. Though we may be tempted to feel sorry for Joseph at this point, the truth is that his trial lingered because God was not yet finished transforming him. God set out to humble Joseph and break his self-life. God wanted to root out Joseph's pride. He had gone from being the "anointed one" whom the entire family would bow down to, to being a common jail bird. Yet, it was all in God's plan and God was with him.

After a few years in prison, Joseph began to submit to God. Two of his fellow inmates, a butler of the king and the king's baker, were also on trial. The Lord showed Joseph through a dream what the outcome of their sentencing would be. Joseph spoke to the butler and asked him to remember him when he was set free, and to please speak to Pharaoh about his situation (Genesis 40:14). This request was evidence that Joseph had not yet learned to fully rely on God. He was still relying on the arm of the flesh. Joseph had passed some tests, but there were still other things God must work in his character before he was ready to be elevated. When the butler was acquitted, he forgot about Joseph (Genesis 40:23).

The forty-first chapter of Genesis begins with the phrase "at the end of two full years." We are told that Joseph was in prison for two full years after he asked for the butler's assistance. As was the case in the life of Joseph, there are things in our lives that God needs to teach us that will only be done in time. God's goal for Joseph's life was for him to be a great man and reign over the nation, but during his extended stay in jail, it didn't look like that would ever be a reality. This is why we cannot look at where we are as evidence of what God has in mind for us.

*For I know the plans that I have for you... thoughts of peace and
not evil.*

Jeremiah 29:11

The last two years of Joseph's imprisonment brought him to true
humility. God had broken the false adequacy off of his life, and he
was learning to fully rely on God. Then at the appropriate time, Pharaoh had a dream and the dream greatly disturbed him. Everyone was
concerned about this dream that the Pharaoh had. It was at this time
(God's time) that the butler remembered Joseph (Genesis 41:9-13).

It was not coincidence that the butler forgot Joseph; it was the
working of God. In God's perfect timing, the butler remembered!
How many times have we forced things to happen that were not within the timing of the Father? At just the right time, the butler told
Pharaoh that while he was in prison Joseph interpreted his dream.
Pharaoh sends for Joseph (Genesis 41:14). Notice closely the dialog
between the Pharaoh and Joseph:

> *And the Pharaoh said unto Joseph, I have dreamed a dream, and
> there is none that can interpret it: and I have heard say of thee,
> that thou canst understand a dream to interpret it. And Joseph an-
> swered the Pharaoh, saying, It is not in me, God shall give Pharaoh
> an answer of peace.*
>
> Genesis 41:15-16

When we think of what the natural response to Pharaoh's statement would be, it would make sense for Joseph to say, "Hey Pharaoh,
I sure can interpret your dream; that is my ministry. I can do this!" But
that would be the response of a man full of false adequacy. Joseph was
now a man who had had false adequacy broken from over his life. This
is why he replies, "I cannot do it...It is not in me...If God does not do

it, it will not be done." Joseph's time in prison had shaped in him the character that God was looking for. This Joseph, not the old one, was what God desired. God is looking for that man today who will give Him the glory and the praise for what is done in his life.

Joseph's words show that his training was complete, he was ready to reign. Joseph listened to Pharaoh's dream and interpreted it. Two years earlier, when Joseph spoke to the butler and asked him to speak to Pharaoh for him, he was not yet broken. But now Joseph was broken. He stood before Pharaoh himself, but he knew enough not to dare speak out of his own strength or intelligence. This was a new Joseph.

After Joseph interpreted the dream, he told Pharaoh that he needed to seek a man to oversee the management of his resources because God was going to send a famine. Joseph did not pitch for the job. Joseph realized that he was in the hand of the Lord.

> *Now let Pharaoh look out a man discreet and wise, and set him over the land of Egypt. Let Pharaoh do this.*
>
> Genesis 41:33-34

Joseph humbled himself under the mighty hand of God and waited. He did not realize that the time of his exaltation had come. Pharaoh said to Joseph:

> *For as much as God has shewed thee all this, there is none so discreet and wise as thou art. Thou shalt be over my house, and according unto thy word shall all my people be ruled: only in the throne will I be greater than thou.*
>
> Genesis 41: 39-40

Joseph had died to himself and had learned to truly yield to God. His elevation was evidence of his brokenness. I think it is important to say here that in a generation where everyone is seeking spiritual elevation, we must humble ourselves and realize that success is God's to give us, not ours to take.

Once we humble ourselves, we realize that successful ministers and pastors have been blessed by God with success. It is a false assumption to believe that by human efforts we can secure what truly only God can grant. God knows when and where we need to be elevated. Too many of God's people are vainly seeking to match their brother's or sister's success without the consent of God. This is futile! I am writing today while the nations are commemorating the death of Nelson Mandela of South Africa. This great man, Nelson Mandela, was a modern day Joseph!

Joseph and Jacob

After many years, Joseph came into his inheritance that he only dreamed about many years before. He was now mature in God. He was the Prince of Egypt. No longer walking in pride, he had learned to trust God. Through many trials and struggles, he entered into his destiny. There was famine in the land, but Egypt had food because of the wisdom and anointing of Joseph.

People came from all over the known world to Egypt to find food. Jacob (Israel) and his family were constrained by the famine. Jacob sent his sons to Egypt to find provision (Genesis 42:1-3). When Joseph's brothers came before him, they bowed down. They were not aware that this Prince of Egypt was their little brother. They were convinced that Joseph was dead. Joseph commanded his brothers to go back home and bring their younger brother back to present himself before him. Joseph secretly had the money they had brought to pay for grain placed back into their sacks. He also gave them food for their journey. This evidences the fact that Joseph was walking in love. He did not carry bitterness, resentment, or prejudice in his heart against his brothers. You cannot reign with these things in your heart.

The brothers returned and told their father what had happened. The old Jacob would have devised some trickery against the prince. But this man was no longer Jacob, he was Israel. He had learned to operate in God's strength, and not his own strength. He had learned to be righteous and gracious.

He sent the money back to Joseph, asserting that its inclusion in their sacks may have been an oversight. Israel also sent Benjamin as Joseph requested, and by faith he declared the protection of God over his sons (Genesis 43:11-14). He inclined himself to do what was right and not walk in the way of trickery. Israel sent with his sons the best from his land as a gift to the prince. His thinking had been transformed from a selfish trickery to a godly standard. He did not operate the way he once did. He was now Israel, and he knew how to do things God's way.

After the brothers returned to Egypt with their youngest brother, Benjamin, they were accused of stealing Joseph's cup. But Joseph could not continue the ruse. He broke down because of the great love in his heart, and told them that he was their brother.

One would think that after the long and arduous life Joseph lived, he might have devised a plot for revenge. But Joseph had been transformed by God. Through his trials, God had perfected Joseph's character. He showed mercy to the very brothers who sold him into slavery. The natural mind would only have harbored hatred. But Joseph's words for his brothers were:

Now therefore, be not grieved, nor angry with yourselves, that ye sold me hither: for God did send me before you to preserve (your) life.

Genesis 45:5 (explanation mine)

Such gracious words could only be the product of a changed life. God is in the business of changing Jacobs to Israels, of changing self-centered Josephs into the Prince of Egypt. All this is done through the transformation of one's character.

Joseph's brothers returned to Israel to testify that Joseph was alive. The natural man—Jacob—did not believe the words of his sons, but the spiritual man—Israel—was eventually able to rejoice.

And they told (Jacob) saying, Joseph is yet alive, and he is the governor over all the land of Egypt. And Jacob's heart fainted, for he believed them not.

Genesis 45:26

After seeing the wagons which Joseph had sent to carry him back to Egypt, Jacob's faith was invigorated.

And Israel said, It is enough; Joseph my son is yet alive; I will go and see him before I die.

Genesis 45:28

There is a Jacob in all of us; it is our flesh. There is also a spiritual man, an Israel, in us all. As we learn to die to ourselves and live in the spirit, we will experience the transformation of the Lord and the fulfillment of all His promises.

These stories of these three biblical characters— Mephibosheth, Jacob, and Joseph—were meant for our example. We must each examine ourselves to recognize the roots of false adequacy in our own lives and break free of its bondage.

Chapter 7

Glorify God

The purpose behind embracing our inadequacy is so that God will get the glory in all things. If we admit we are insufficient and turn to Him as our sufficiency, we will glorify Him for the things He does for us and call Him Lord. Conversely, if we feel that we are sufficient within ourselves, we will give God only cursory acknowledgement for being our Creator. If we believe that somehow we are adequate, we will withhold all the praise, honor, and glory that belong to God. Therefore, God is always demonstrating to us our insufficiencies so that we may become humble enough to praise Him.

Today the "American Idol" is that of bringing glory to self. This is the same sin that the wicked one committed in heaven.

> *How art thou fallen from heaven, O Lucifer, son of the morning! how art thou cut down to the ground, which didst weaken the nations! For thou hast said in thine heart, I will ascend into heaven, I will exalt my throne above the stars of God: I will also sit upon the mount of the congregation, in the sides of the north: I will ascend above the heights of the clouds; I will be like the most High. Yet thou shalt be brought down to hell, to the sides of the pit.*
>
> Isaiah 14:12-15

Our assignment on this earth is not to show people how special or capable we are, nor to bring credit and recognition and glory to ourselves.

Our assignment on this earth is to bring glory to God. The phrase, "glorify His name" is used a lot in Scripture. To "glorify His name" means to cause one to think so highly of God that he feels compelled to worship God. "To glorify God" also means to cause God to be favored among men; to cause men to acknowledge and to know Him. The great work of the Church and of the saints is that of glorifying God.

"The Glory of God" vs. "Glorifying God"

Surely God is interested in His glory. It is one of His highest concerns. The Bible speaks of both "the glory of God" and "glorifying God," yet there is a significant difference between the two. We do well to recognize this subtle difference in Scripture. What is the glory of God? It is who God is; it is the essence of His nature, the weight of His importance, the radiance of His splendor, the demonstration of His power, and the atmosphere of His presence. God is awesome! To be in His presence is beyond anything that we can imagine!

In the Bible, Moses asked God to give him a glimpse of His glory.

And he said, I beseech thee, show me thy glory.

Exodus 33:18

In His mercy, God replied,

Thou canst not see my face, for there shall no man see me and live. Behold there is a place by me, and thou shalt stand upon a rock: and it shall come to pass, while my glory passeth by, that I will put thee in the cleft of the rock, and I will cover thee with my hand while I pass by: And I will take away my hand, and thou shalt see my back parts: but my face shall not be seen.

Exodus 33:18-23

After Moses witnessed the back parts of God's glory, he came down from the mountain to the people of Israel.

When he came down from the mount, Moses knew not that his face glowed.

Exodus 34:29

The glory of God had been imparted on the person of Moses. This displaced glory just from the back parts of the presence of God was so powerful that Moses had to put a veil over his face.

And till Moses had done speaking with the people, he put a veil on his face.

Exodus 34:33

This story clearly demonstrates the glory of God. But what does it mean to "glorify God?" Glorifying God simply means bringing recognition and acclaim to Him. Our job as ambassadors of heaven living on the earth is to glorify our Heavenly King. We are not on this earth to live for our desires. We are here to glorify God.

Unfinished Business

It is time that we, as God's children, become sensitive to this one truth: God is the only One who deserves the glory. We are His children and we are blessed to call ourselves the sons and daughters of God (1 John 3:1-2). However, we must understand that we do not deserve the glory. In fact, God is collecting His glory from those who have stolen it.

We need to give God the glory for any blessing in our lives that has come to us by the direct imposition of His grace and mercy. Giving

God glory through praise and worship is the currency we use to make payment to the Father for all He has done in our lives. He is due glory daily for the many blessings He has bestowed on us.

We can rob God in the tithe, but we can also rob God in worship. In Luke Chapter 17, we have the story of the miracle of the healing of the ten lepers. These ten leprous men exercised their faith by being obedient to Jesus' command to go see the priest (Luke 17:14). As this great healing manifested, one of the men recognized that there was still some unfinished business—he was responsible to give honor to God for the healing that He had done in his life.

> *And one of them, when he saw that he was healed, turned back, and with a loud voice glorified God and fell down on his face at his feet, giving him thanks.*
>
> Luke 17:15-16

Jesus verified that this man did the right thing in giving glory to God. When the man fell down at Jesus' feet in profuse praise, Jesus replied:

> *Were there not ten cleansed? But where are the nine? There are not found that returned to give glory to God, save this stranger.*
>
> Luke 17:17-18

This man knew he owed God praise and thanks, and Jesus also knew that he owed glory to God. Unfortunately, many believers today do not know that they owe glory to God. God's glory is a great unpaid debt in our churches today. God will bless us with the things we ask for in prayer, but God expects us to recognize that once we receive that blessing, there is still some unfinished business. We can have the new car, but we cannot have the glory. We can have the house, but we cannot have the glory. We can have the position or promotion, but we cannot have the glory. We can have the spiritual gift, but we cannot have the glory. We can have the ministry, but we cannot have the glory.

We get in trouble when we refuse to render glory to God for the benefits we receive. Therefore, our confession must be, "God, if You give me the blessing, I will give You the glory." Don't ever get caught with God's glory still in your mouth.

By (Jesus) therefore let us offer the sacrifice of praise to God contin-
ually, that is, the fruit of our lips giving thanks to His name.

Hebrews 13:15 (explanation mine)

We must learn to praise God for all of our blessings. When we fail to give praise, we are stealing the glory. God does not share His glory!

I am the LORD, that is my name; and my glory I will not give to
another, nor my praise to carved image.

Isaiah 42:8

Since God made all things, He deserves all the glory. David was correct when he wrote:

I will bless the LORD at all times, his praise shall continually be in
my mouth.

Psalm 34:1

Why Worship?

Offer unto God thanksgiving; and pay thy vows unto the most
High: and call upon me in the day of trouble: I will deliver thee,
and thou shalt glorify me.

Psalm 50:14-15

Give unto the LORD the glory due unto his name: bring an offering,
and come before him: worship the LORD in the beauty of holiness.

1 Chronicles 16:29

Worship is our first responsibility to God. Worship should be the centerpiece of our lives. If we do not worship God, there is some form of false adequacy that is attached to our lives. Every believer must come to realize that it is his responsibility to glorify God. We bring glory to God by worshipping Him for who He is and praising Him for the things He has done. Yet, too many believers do not know the glory of our God, and many do not give glory to Him. But God is dealing with His people. God is collecting His glory.

How much have you glorified God this week? How much praise and worship has come from your mouth? How much have you given monetarily to God this month? The Bible says:

Honor the LORD with thy substance, and with the firstfruits of all
thine increase.

Proverbs 3:9

This scripture is talking about our responsibility to glorify God by offering thanksgiving, paying vows, and worshipping the Lord. These are three ways we give glory to God. Man needs deliverance, and God desires glory. If man will offer praise and thanksgiving to God and pay his tithes and offering, then God declares that He will do His part. What is God's part? God's part is to deliver us when we are in trouble.

The scripture from 1 Chronicles 16 speaks of giving God the glory due His name. This implies that someone has God's glory and is reluctant to give it to Him. Who has God's glory? Those who have been blessed by God—you and I have God's glory!

Where is God's glory? It is in our mouth. Our responsibility as believers is to render unto God the glory due His name. Yet most of us are behind on our praise because we have been impressed with ourselves. When God delivers us from false adequacy, we will rise up in our spirit man and give Him the glory due His name.

People often say, "I go to this or that church because I enjoy the worship." This statement is in error. Worship was never meant for us. Worship was meant for God. In order for one to truly become a worshipper, we must commit to a lifestyle of worship that pleases God. The modern mind assumes that everything is for "me." But glorifying God requires the renunciation of "me" and the exaltation of "He."

False adequacy makes us believe we should enjoy the style of worship. Instead, we should pray that God would enjoy the worship. When is the last time you made the heavens and the earth and so were worthy of worship? When God breaks false adequacy from over our lives, we will be able to assume our proper place in the worship of God.

Spiritual Shoplifters

Praise, worship, and thanksgiving are choices that each believer must make. God does not force man to worship Him. Man must choose to worship and honor their heavenly Father. Worship is a debt we owe to God for the many blessings He has afforded us. But in many believers' lives, this debt goes unpaid.

When you walk into a department store, *you* choose your items and *you* take them to the checkout for purchase. At the checkout, *you* pay with money for the items *you* chose. Those people who choose items within the store but fail to go by the checkout line and pay for them are called "shoplifters."

In the same way, God has a storehouse of blessing. We enter into His Kingdom through salvation and we reap the benefits of salvation through our prayers. However, when we claim these blessings, we are to go by the checkout to pay for our blessings. But we do not pay with money; we pay God with our worship, praise, and thanksgiving.

Many believers have secured the blessings of God without going through the checkout line. They are "spiritual shoplifters." They are looking for the next blessing without realizing that the Sheriff is looking for them. They have violated spiritual law by not "paying" for their first blessings. Their status in the spirit realm is criminal because they have neglected to tender the worship, praise and thanksgiving God is due.

By him therefore let us offer the sacrifice of praise to God continually, that is, the fruit of our lips giving thanks to his name.

Hebrews 13:15

The Anatomy of a Miracle

Throughout the Bible, God performs many miracles. The Old Testament scriptures are replete with stories of God taking great pains to ensure the inadequacy of those participating in the miracle. Let's take David's bout with Goliath as an example. David is a very young man when he endeavors to fight Goliath. David does not wear King Saul's armor when he goes out to fight Goliath (1 Samuel 17:39). Furthermore, David only takes with him a staff, a sling, and five stones into the battle (1 Samuel 17:40). These conditions were required so we would not view David as adequate to defeat Goliath. Yet, despite his inadequacy, God gives David victory.

Next, let us consider Gideon. Gideon was the lowest member of the poorest family in Israel (Judges 6:15). This ensured that he would be viewed by the people as socially inadequate. Furthermore, while Gideon started his campaign against the Midianites with over thirty thousand men, he was commanded by God to only take 300 men with him into battle (Judges 7:2-6). This ensured that the victory would not be won by the adequacy of the strength of men. God confirmed this when He said to Gideon:

> *The people that are with thee are too many for me to give the Midianites into their hands, lest Israel vaunt themselves against me, saying, mine own hand hath saved me.*

Judges 7:2

Now let us consider Moses. God chose a man who was slow of speech to ensure that we would not be impressed with his eloquence. Moses himself was convinced that he was inadequate to match wits with Pharaoh.

> *And Moses said unto God, Who am I, that I should go unto Pharaoh.*

Exodus 3:11

We can also recall the battles of the Israelites in the books of Samuel, Kings, and Chronicles where God delivered His people in situations where they were greatly outnumbered or disadvantaged. This left them with no doubt that it was God who secured the victory. All throughout the Bible, God takes great pains to ensure that man looks weak, so that He looks great. God is determined not to make much of us, but to make much of Himself. God does not seek to make man look great. God seeks to make Himself look like he is the Real Deal! God actually delights in exalting our inability and insufficiency so that we become more and more dependent upon Him.

But we have this treasure in earthen vessels, that the excellency of the power may be of God, and not of us.

2 Corinthians 4:7

God intentionally allows His people to encounter situations where they come face to face with their need for His assistance. This is why anyone who is living by a philosophy of 'I need God minimally' is deceived by false adequacy. God wants to do great things through us, but we must first be convinced of our own insufficiency. Once we are thoroughly convinced that we cannot do things without God, we can simply rest in Him and wait for His salvation.

God wants to demonstrate to His people, His ability to provide everything they need in ways they could never have mustered up or imagined. God, when dealing with the Israelites in the wilderness, waited until the people were so hungry or thirsty that they cried out before He intervened (Exodus 17:1-3). This is because only when we are convinced of our own inadequacy, will we be totally dependent upon God. As long as there is some strength or some ingenuity within us, we will seek to provide for ourselves. But when we come to the end of our "self," God can be perfectly glorified.

And he said unto me, My grace is sufficient for thee: for my strength is made perfect in weakness. Most gladly therefore will I rather glory in my infirmities, that the power of Christ may rest upon me.

2 Corinthians 12:9

God allows people to get into positions where they desperately need His power, His might, His healing, His provision, and His deliverance, so that He might show Himself to be El Shaddai. Some saints are in desperate circumstances today, but they still have not acknowledged their need for God. There is still a seed of false adequacy resident in them. Only when they are convinced that they cannot produce, will God add His strength.

I am learning on a personal level just how inadequate I am. My biggest challenge is learning to embrace my insufficiencies and inadequacies. In a world where everyone is seeking to show how exceptional they are, God is looking for those who can embrace their inadequacy.

Therefore, I take pleasure in infirmities, in reproaches, in necessities, in persecution, in distresses for Christ sake: for when I am weak, then I am strong.

2 Corinthians 12:10

Misdirected Glory

And all the people brake off the golden earrings which were in their ears, and brought them unto Aaron. And he received them at their hand, and fashioned it with a graving tool, after he had made it a molten calf: and they said, these be thy gods, O Israel, which brought thee up out of the land of Egypt.

Exodus 32:3-4

God delivered the Israelites from their bondage in Egypt and from the armies of the Pharaoh, and brought them through the Red Sea. Yet after all this, they decided that the credit for all this deliverance did not belong to God. The Israelites instead made a golden calf and gave it the credit and the glory for bringing them out of Egypt.

Nehemiah offers commentary on the mindset and actions of the Israelites in the wilderness. He writes:

(God) gavest them bread from heaven for their hunger, and broughtest forth water for them out of the rock for their thirst, and promisedst them that they should go in to possess the land which thou hadst sworn to give them. But they and our fathers dealt proudly, and hardened their necks, and hearkened not to thy commandments, and refused to obey, neither were mindful of thy wonders that thou didst among them; but hardened their necks and in their rebellion appointed a captain to return to their bondage.

Nehemiah 9:15-17

Notice that the commentary of Nehemiah says that they "dealt proudly" against God. It is pride that hinders one from worshipping God. We cannot praise God until we have been delivered from pride. Pride is the root of false adequacy. Once there is pride in us, we are apt to find someone or something other than God to give the glory to. Often we give credit and glory to ourselves, to fate, or to other people for the things God has done for us.

Nehemiah further writes:

But thou art a God ready to pardon, gracious and merciful, slow to anger, and of great kindness, and forsook them not.

Nehemiah 9:17

Thank God for His humility. In our false adequacy, we often give ourselves the credit and glory for what God has done in our lives. Yet God never leaves us, nor forsakes us. The world might be confused about Who sends the rain, but the saints should not be. It is time we become better witnesses to the goodness of the Lord.

David's Worship

*I will bless the LORD at all times; his praise shall continually be in
my mouth. My soul shall make her boast in the LORD: the humble
shall hear thereof and be glad. O magnify the LORD with me, and
let us exalt his name together.*

Psalm 34:1-3

*I will praise the name of God with a song, and will magnify Him
with thanksgiving. This also shall please the LORD better than an
ox or bullock that hath horns and hoofs. The humble shall see this,
and be glad: and your heart shall live that seek God.*

Psalm 69:30-32

In both the scriptures above, there is a subtle implication that only
the humble will worship God. Notice it says, *"The humble shall hear
thereof..." "The humble shall see this..."* Could it be that the thing that
God appreciated most about David was his humility?

David was a man after God's own heart (Acts 13:22). When we
hear this, we are inclined to believe that he did everything right. But
this is not the case, by David's own admission. If he didn't do everything right, then why would God give David such a high honor? I
believe it's because David had one thing right: He had the humility to
recognize his own inadequacy.

David was a worshipper and worship implies that one recognizes
his need for God. Many people do not worship God because they are
not yet fully convinced that they need Him. Others may be ashamed
to worship God before men. But Jesus has already informed us that the
seed of shame before men will bring a harvest of Jesus being ashamed
of us before the Father in heaven (Mark 8:38).

Many believers have embraced the Bible as truth. They love Sunday school, church, and religious events. They study the Bible religiously, but still have not embraced worship. One can be a teacher of the Word of God and still not be a worshipper. One can be a choir member and still not be a worshipper. One can be a leader in the church and still not be a worshipper.

Many wither at the thought of other people seeing them worship. This is why it takes humility to be a worshipper. One has to resolve that he will not be moved by the opinions and values of other people. In order to worship, we must become less impressed with other people's opinion than God's opinion of us. Only then will we become like David. God is looking for those who will lift up holy hands and give Him praise!

True Worshippers

Ye worship ye know not what: we know what we worship: for salvation is of the Jews. But the hour cometh, and now is, when the true worshippers shall worship the Father in spirit and in truth: for the Father seeketh such to worship him. God is a Spirit: and they that worship him must worship him in spirit and in truth.

John 4:22-24

Jesus did not tell the woman at the well that God was looking for Bible students. He told her that the Father was seeking worshippers. Worship glorifies and pleases God. Therefore, we can be sure that when we worship God, He recognizes our offering. Worship is the only area where the weakest or poorest saint can make a greater offering than the well-endowed.

There are many people today who are seeking God for one thing or another. However, there are a few people whom God is seeking. True worshipers don't have to seek God…God seeks them. When we commit our lives to worship—when His praise is in our mouth—He will come to us. We don't have to deliver God's glory to Him; He'll come and pick it up!

God is a Spirit and his interactions with us are never with our flesh. We do not relate to God through our flesh. Genesis 5:17 says, *"The flesh lusts against the spirit and the spirit against the flesh."* By this we know that the flesh and the spirit never fellowship with one another. Since God is a Spirit, He will only fellowship with our spirit.

Too often we look at worship from the perspective of the flesh. We hear the music, we raise our hands, we sing the songs, but these things are not worship. Then what is worship, you may ask? Worship is the honor that comes forth out of your spirit while you are singing or raising your hands. You can sing the song, raise your hands, or play the music with no intention to honor the Father. The "true worshipper" that Jesus speaks of is what we must seek to become. If our worship is to be pleasing to God, we must get in touch with our spirit. Our worship offering must proceed forth out of the purity of our spirit. Then as we commit ourselves to worship God from our spirit, He will be glorified in our lives.

"Glory-Seeking"

One of the idols that we, as Americans, deal with today is the belief that we are destined for greatness. Our culture has impressed upon us the false idea that we deserve greatness and glory. As believers, the view that we are destined for greatness is a great weight and a hindrance to our service to God. We must change the mentality of "I am great" to a new reality of "I am destined to make Him great."

Many believers desire the prestige and honor that comes with being a minister or pastor. As a young minister, the idol I dealt with was that I wanted to be a successful pastor, but I was measuring this by a worldly definition of success. Since I had been called to preach, I assumed that I had the "right" to aspire to be a person who ministers to thousands. I was busy building my own kingdom while using God's name. What I was actually doing is called "glory-seeking." The Bible speaks much of glory-seeking.

> *Let nothing be done through strife or vainglory.*
>
> Philippians 2:3

Do you know what "vainglory" is? It is doing ministry with a view towards being applauded and acknowledged by men. Vainglory is another word for glory-seeking. Jesus had this vanity in mind when He said,

> *How can you believe, which receive honor one of another, and seek not the honor that comes from God only.*
>
> John 5:44

Glory-seeking has everything to do with our motivation for doing ministry. If our motivation for ministry is centered on bringing recognition to ourselves or obtaining the acknowledgement and praise of men, then we are glory-seeking.

> *For neither at any time used we flattering words, as ye know, nor a cloak of covetousness; God is witness: Nor of men sought we glory, neither of you, nor yet of others.*
>
> 1 Thessalonians 2:5-6

Have you ever seen someone minister and got the feeling that they were overly interested in promoting themselves? Over the years, televised ministry has spoiled many men and women of God. Our pursuit to be like the ministers on television has weakened our desire to be more like Jesus.

It's the same way in many of our churches today. We get so busy pushing for numbers because we falsely assume that God is as impressed with crowds as we are. But remember, Jesus often ministered to just one person: the woman at the well, Zacchaeus, Blind Bartimaeus, and many others. We must constantly remind ourselves that the glory for ministry must never come to us. If a church is large, it is large to the glory of God. If a church is small, it is small to the glory of God. Whatever God puts in our hands to do, let us do it to the glory of God!

Herod's Oration

And upon a set day Herod, arrayed in royal apparel, set upon his throne, and made an oration unto them. And the people gave a shout, saying, It is the voice of a god, and not of a man. And immediately the angel of the Lord smote him, because he gave not God the glory: and he was eaten of worms, and gave up the ghost. But the word of God grew and multiplied.

Acts 12:21-24

This is a very important story in the Bible. It speaks of a great oration or speech that was made by King Herod. It also notes that Herod was "arrayed in royal apparel" when he made this speech. It was one of his finest moments. The men who heard the speech were impressed. They said things like, "It is the voice of a god!" I can just imagine Herod strutting around, drinking up the glory juice. But the verse says that the angel of the Lord smote Herod because he did not give God the glory.

This story shows us how serious stealing God's glory is. We are ambassadors for Christ and spokesmen for God, yet we must be careful that we are not speaking for God without acknowledging that the power for ministry comes from the Spirit of God and that the glory of ministry must return to God. We sing under the anointing. We teach under the anointing. We heal under the anointing. Yet, all the glory belongs to God!

Once I was talking to a woman who was a gifted gospel singer. She expressed to me that in her heart she really wanted to sing for God. She said, "I can just see myself walking out on that stage in front of thousands of people shouting and clapping for me." To most of us, we see this sort of expression as normal. After all, we think, shouldn't she have high aspirations for herself? However, such a thought reveals a person who is totally insensitive to her responsibility to glorify God.

In my ambition to be a pastor and to have a big church, I never stopped to ask the simple question: *Am I seeking to become the pastor of a big church for God's glory or for my own recognition?* Now, if I am truly seeking God's glory and God's glory alone, it does not matter what or where God uses me, as long as He is satisfied and glorified. However, my aspirations were very selfish, even though the entire time I thought I was doing God's will.

The modern-day concept of glorifying God includes glorifying ourselves. We tell ourselves, "God is going to look good, because I am going to look good." The modern mind cannot fathom the idea that we can look bad, while God looks good. But that is the biblical imperative that the men and women of God lived by. John the Baptist said,

I must decrease and he must increase.

John 3:30

Paul the Apostle spoke of it this way:

For we which live are always delivered unto death for Jesus' sake, that the life also of Jesus might be made manifest in our mortal flesh. So then death worketh in us, but life in you.

2 Corinthians 4:11-12

This is where our modern generation has totally disconnected from our responsibility to glorify God. Many saints are vainly seeking their own glory and the worship of God has suffered tremendously as a result. We have tied ourselves so much to God's glory, that we do not understand that we have no right to look good. We erroneously believe that God should be happy with the fragments of our own glory we choose to share. God does not want to make us look good. We are concerned about our clothing, our title, the type of car we drive, the size of our ministry, and so many other fleshly things. We are more concerned with the elevation of our own name than with the glory of our God's name.

If any man speak, let him speak as the oracles of God; if any man minister, let him do it as of the ability which God giveth: that God in all things may be glorified through Jesus Christ, to whom be praise and dominion forever and ever. Amen.

1 Peter 4:11

Over the years, God has taught me that glory-seeking is a desire that other people recognize our virtues, gifts, and talents; all of which have been given to us by God. Many believers have forgotten that their gifts are endowments from God, and spiritual gifts are actually tools that God gives us to accomplish His purpose on the earth. Too many believers become prideful when they recognize that they are gifted in some way.

For who maketh thee to differ from another? And what hast thou that thou didst not receive (from God)? Now if thou didst receive it, why dost thou glory, as if thou hadst not received it?

1 Corinthians 4:7 (explanation mine)

If God has gifted you, why do you act like you made yourself good at what you do? When you are glory-seeking instead of glorifying God, you minister with a view towards promoting yourself. Most glory-seeking ministers do not realize that they are glory-seeking. The idea of self-promotion is so woven into their thoughts that they believe that it is normal—even godly.

Early one morning, at twilight, God spoke to me and said, "Your job is to glorify Me!" I was confused. It set me back for a season because that's exactly what I thought I had been doing. I was preaching salvation through Jesus Christ and teaching God's Word. In actuality, however, I was completely obsessed with my own glory. Because I was glory-seeking, I resented other ministers. I saw them as the competition. My resentment for other ministries was evidence that I was glory-seeking. All of this glory-seeking was the outworking of my own pride and self-life.

When we try to elevate and promote ourselves, we lose a lot of money and time. For instance, I paid for television ministry for years without asking God if it was His will for my life. My desire to elevate in ministry drove me. I was working slavishly to build my own ministry. My motives were self-serving. I did not ask God to give me a ministry; firstly, because I did not trust Him to bless me with a ministry, and secondly, because if He gave me a ministry, I would deserve no recognition. Because we do much with glory-seeking in mind, we become insensitive to the fact that we care very little about the will of God or the glory of God.

> *And the loftiness of man shall be bowed down, and the haughtiness of men shall be made low: and the LORD alone shall be exalted in that day.*
>
> Isaiah 2:17

In order for God to be glorified in our lives, we must first realize that it is our responsibility to glorify Him. Just speaking of glorifying God does not glorify Him. If a believer wants to do his part in glorifying God, he must first consciously diminish himself. Our flesh naturally desires to aggrandize and bring honor to itself. But those of us who have humbled ourselves and come to the realization that we are inadequate and deserve no glory, are now ready to give the glory to the One who rightfully deserves it.

Self-Diminishment

In a world where everyone seeks to show themselves as great, we condition ourselves to live a life that shows that Jesus Christ is great. I call this self-diminishment. This means living life with the self-effacing mentality that the Lord Jesus is more important than we are. Now this certainly does not mean that there are not moments when it is appropriate to honor human accomplishments. We must not be so full of false modesty that we cannot accept or offer a compliment. What self-diminshment actually means is living with a deliberate consciousness of worshiping and bringing honor to God, rather than elevating ourselves. It means remembering to say, "God did this for me," instead of "I did it." This brings glory to God. We must decrease, so that God may increase. Self-diminishment, a type of humility, must become a deliberate practice in the Body of Christ.

Let nothing be done through strife or vainglory; but in lowliness of mind let each esteem other better than themselves.

Philippians 2:3

Decreasing means denying the honor that comes from affluence. It means putting in an offering on Sunday morning without recognition. Self-diminishment means living the life God has called us to live, not the life we have chosen for ourselves.

The woman of Samaria is a good example of self-diminishment. She was obviously a very beautiful woman. Jesus said that she had had five husbands and number six was in the making (John 4:18). This woman's beauty apparently drew men to her, but when Jesus taught her about worship, it caused her to see her own inadequacy (John 4:20-24). The revelation of worship changed her perspective and helped her to see that she should not be the center of attention. Formerly, she used her beauty to draw men to herself but with this new perspective, she diminished herself and caused men to see their need for Jesus.

And many of the Samaritans of that city believed on him for the saying of the woman, which testified.

John 4:39

There are many in the Kingdom who have become too big for their britches. There are those in the Kingdom who are so worldly, they see self-aggrandizing as normal and natural. Taking up your cross means dying to this world and the glory of it. Taking up your cross means crucifying self so that Jesus Christ can shine through. My brothers and sisters, we are not American Idols, we are the children of God in a foreign land. Let us glorify God during this short season while we are on this earth and God will reward us for our service when we return home.

Prayer: *Father, glorify Yourself in me and through me. My life is an instrument of Your glory. Teach me how I can bring You glory among the saved as well as the unsaved. I renounce a selfish life. I no longer seek my own glory. I no longer seek my own will. I no longer live my own way. Death to me and glory to You. Amen.*

Scriptures on Pride

The wicked in his pride doth persecute the poor: let them be taken in the devices that they have imagined.

Psalm 10:2

*The fear of the L*ORD *is to hate evil: pride and arrogancy, and the evil way, and the froward mouth, do I hate.*

Proverbs 8:13

Let not the foot of pride come against me, and let not the hand of the wicked remove me.

Psalm 36:11

When pride cometh, then cometh shame: but with the lowly is wisdom.

Proverbs 11:2

Only by pride cometh contention: but with the well advised is wisdom.

Proverbs 13:10

Pride goeth before destruction, and a haughty spirit before a fall.

Proverbs 16:18

A man's pride shall bring him low: but honor shall uphold the humble in spirit.

Proverbs 29:23

Thus saith the LORD, *After this manner will I mar the pride of Judah, and the great pride of Jerusalem.*

Jeremiah 13:9

Thy terribleness hath deceived thee, and the pride of thine heart, O thou that dwellest in the clefts of the rock, that holdest the height of the hill: though thou shouldest make thy nest as high as the eagle, I will bring thee down from thence, saith the LORD.

Jeremiah 49:16

Now I Nebuchadnezzar praise and extol and honor the King of heaven, all whose works are truth, and his ways judgment: and those that walk in pride he is able to abase.

Daniel 4:37

Not a novice, lest being lifted up with pride he fall into the condemnation of the devil.

1 Timothy 3:6

For all that is in the world, the lust of the flesh, and the lust of the eyes, and the pride of life, is not of the Father, but is of the world.

1 John 2:16

These six things doth the LORD *hate: yea seven are an abomination unto him: A proud look, a lying tongue, and hands that shed innocent blood.*

Proverbs 6:16–17

An high look, and a proud heart, and the plowing of the wicked, is sin.

Proverbs 21:4

Every one that is proud in heart is an abomination to the LORD: *though hand join in hand, he shall not be unpunished.*

Proverbs 16:5

He hath shewed strength with his arm; he hath scattered the proud in the imagination of their hearts.

Luke 1:51

He is proud, knowing nothing, but doting about questions and strifes of words, whereof cometh envy, strife, railings, evil surmising.

1 Timothy 6:4

Vainly puffed up by his fleshy mind...

Colossians 2:18

And Samuel said, When thou was little in thine own sight, wast thou not made head of the tribes of Israel, and the LORD *anointed thee king over Israel?*

For rebellion is as the sin of witchcraft, and stubbornness is as iniquity and idolatry. Because thou hast rejected the word of the LORD, *he hath also rejected thee from being king.*

1 Samuel 15:17, 23

Scriptures on Humility

Let this mind be in you, which was also in Christ Jesus: Who being in the form of God, thought it not robbery to be equal with God: but made himself of no reputation, and took upon him the form of a servant, and was made in the likeness of men: And being found in fashion as a man, he humbled himself and became obedient unto death, even the death of the cross. Wherefore God also hath highly exalted him, and given him a name which is above every name: That at the name of Jesus every knee should bow, of things in heaven, and things in earth, and things under the earth; And that every tongue should confess that Jesus Christ is Lord, to the glory of God the Father.

Philippians 2:5-11

But he giveth more grace. Wherefore he saith, God resisteth the proud, but giveth grace unto the humble.

James 4:6

Humble yourselves in the sight of the Lord, and he shall lift you up.

James 4:10

But he that is greatest among you shall be your servant. And whosoever shall exalt himself shall be abased; and he that shall humble himself shall be exalted.

Matthew 23:11-12

Whosoever therefore shall humble himself as this little child, the same is greatest in the kingdom of heaven.

Matthew 18:4

Nevertheless divers of Asher and Manasseh and of Zebulun humbled themselves, and came to Jerusalem.

2 Chronicles 30:11

For whosoever exalteth himself shall be abased; and he that humbleth himself shall be exalted.

Luke 14:11

I tell you, this man went down to his house justified rather than the other: for every one that exalteth himself shall be abased; and he that humbleth himself shall be exalted."

Luke 18:14

Put on therefore, as the elect of God, holy and beloved, bowels of mercies, kindness, humbleness of mind, meekness, longsuffering; forbearing one another, and forgiving one another, if any man have a quarrel against any: even as Christ forgave you, so also do ye.

Colossians 3:12-13

The fear of the LORD is the instruction of wisdom; and before honour is humility.

Proverbs 15:33

Let nothing be done through strife or vainglory; but in lowliness of mind let each esteem other better than themselves.

Philippians 2:3

Before destruction the heart of man is haughty, and before honor is humility.

Proverbs 18:12

*Serving the L*ORD *with all humility of mind, and with many tears, and temptations, which befell me by the lying in wait of the Jews.*

Acts 20:19

*And Moses and Aaron came in unto Pharaoh, and said unto him, Thus saith the L*ORD *God of the Hebrews, How long wilt thou refuse to humble thyself before me? Let my people go that they may serve me.*

Exodus 10:3

I my people, which are called by my name, shall humble themselves, and pray, and seek my face, and turn from their wicked ways; then will I hear from heaven, and will forgive their sin, and will heal their land.

2 Chronicles 7:14

When men are cast down, then thou shalt say, There is lifting up; and he shall save the humble person.

Job 22:29

*Though the L*ORD *be high, yet hath he respect unto the lowly: but the proud he knoweth afar off.*

Psalm 138:6

*Hear ye, and give ear; be not proud: for the L*ORD *hath spoken.*

Jeremiah 13:15

For the day of the LORD *of hosts shall be upon every one that is proud and lofty, and upon every one that is lifted up; and he shall be brought low.*

Isaiah 2:12

And Mary said, My soul doth magnify the Lord, and my spirit hath rejoiced in God my Saviour. For he hath regarded the low estate of his handmaiden: for behold, from henceforth all generations shall call me blessed.

Luke 1:46–48

Scriptures on God's Glory

The heavens declare the glory of God.

Psalm 19:1

And the city had no need of the sun, neither of the moon, to shine in it: for the glory of God did lighten it.

Revelation 21:23

And the Word was made flesh and dwelt among us, (and we beheld his glory, the glory as of the only begotten of the Father,) full of grace and truth.

John 1:14

All have sinned, and come short of the glory of God.

Romans 3:23

Because that, when they knew God, they glorified him not as God, neither were thankful; but became vain in their imaginations, and their foolish heart was darkened. Professing themselves to be wise, they became fools, and changed the glory of the incorruptible God into an image made like to corruptible man, and to birds, and to fourfooted beasts, and creeping things. Wherefore God also gave them up to uncleanness through the lusts of their own hearts, to dishonor their own bodies between themselves: Who changed the truth of God into a lie, and worshipped and served the creature more than the Creator, who is blessed forever. Amen.

Romans 1:21-25

And I will harden Pharaoh's heart, that he shall follow after them; and I will be honoured upon Pharaoh, and upon all his host; that the Egyptians may know that I am the LORD. And they did so.

Exodus 14:4

Whoso offereth praise glorifieth me: and to him that ordereth his conversation aright will I shew the salvation of God.

Psalm 50:23

And I will sanctify my great name, which was profaned among the heathen, which ye have profaned in the midst of them; and the heathen shall know that I am the LORD, saith the LORD GOD, when I shall be sanctified in you before their eyes. For I will take you from among the heathen, and gather you out of all countries, and I will bring you into your own land.

Ezekiel 36:23-24

Be still, and know that I am God: I will be exalted among the heathen, I will be exalted in the earth.

Psalm 46:10

Father, glorify thy name. Then came there a voice from heaven, saying, I have both glorified it and will glorify it again. The people therefore, that stood by, and heard it, said that it thundered: others said, *An angel spake to him. Jesus answered and said, This voice came not because of me, but for your sakes.*

John 12:28-30

Therefore, when he was gone out, Jesus said, Now is the Son of man glorified, and God is glorified in him. If God be glorified in him, God shall also glorify him in himself, and shall straightway glorify him.

John 13:31-32

And whatsoever ye shall ask in my name, that will I do, that the Father may be glorified in the Son.

John 14:13

I have glorified thee on the earth: I have finished the work which thou gavest me to do. And now, O Father, glorify thou me with thine own self with the glory which I had with thee before the world was.

John 17:4-5

Our fathers understood not thy wonders in Egypt; they remembered not the multitude of thy mercies; but provoked him at the sea, even at the Red sea. Nevertheless he saved them for his name's sake, that he might make his mighty power to be known.

Psalm 106:7-8

But I am poor and sorrowful: let thy salvation, O God, set me up on high. I will praise the name of God with a song, and will magnify him with thanksgiving. This also shall please the LORD *better than an ox or bullock that hath horns and hoofs. The humble shall see this, and be glad: and your heart shall live that seek God.*

Psalm 69:29-32

And the LORD *said unto Gideon, The people that are with thee are too many for me to give the Midianites into their hands, lest Israel vaunt themselves against me saying, Mine own hand hath saved me.*

Judges 7:2

Let your light so shine before men, that they may see your good works, and glorify your Father which is in heaven.

Matthew 5:16

And whatsoever ye shall ask in my name, that will I do, that the Father may be glorified in the Son.

John 14:13

That the name of our Lord Jesus Christ may be glorified in you, and ye in him, according to the grace of our God and the Lord Jesus Christ.

2 Thessalonians 1:12

For them that honour me I will honour, and they that despise me shall be lightly esteemed.

1 Samuel 2:30

What? Know ye not that your body is the temple of the Holy Ghost which is in you, which ye have of God, and ye are not your own? For ye are bought with a price: therefore glorify God in your body, and in your spirit, which are God's.

1 Corinthians 6:19-20

Whether therefore ye eat, or drink, or whatsoever ye do, do all to the glory of God.

1 Corinthians 10:31

Give unto the LORD *the glory due unto his name; worship the* LORD *in the beauty of holiness.*

Psalm 29:2

Thou art worthy, O Lord to receive glory and honor and power: for thou hast created all things, and for thy pleasure they are and were created.

Revelation 4:11

Even every one that is called by my name: for I have created him for my glory, I have formed him; yea, I have made him.

Isaiah 43:7

I am the LORD: *that is my name: and my glory I will not give to another, neither my praise to graven images.*

Isaiah 42:8

PRAYER OF SALVATION

God loves you—no matter who you are, no matter what your past. God loves you so much that He gave His one and only begotten Son for you. The Bible tells us that "...whoever believes in Him shall not perish but have eternal life" (John 3:16 NIV). Jesus laid down His life and rose again so that we could spend eternity with Him in heaven and experience His absolute best on earth. If you would like to receive Jesus into your life, say the following prayer out loud and mean it from your heart.

Heavenly Father, I come to You admitting that I am a sinner. Right now, I choose to turn away from sin, and I ask You to cleanse me of all unrighteousness. I believe that Your Son, Jesus, died on the cross to take away my sins. I also believe that He rose again from the dead so that I might be forgiven of my sins and made righteous through faith in Him. I call upon the name of Jesus Christ to be the Savior and Lord of my life. Jesus, I choose to follow You and ask that You fill me with the power of the Holy Spirit. I declare that right now I am a child of God. I am free from sin and full of the righteousness of God. I am saved in Jesus' name. Amen.

If you prayed this prayer to receive Jesus Christ as your Savior for the first time, please contact us on the Web at **www.harrisonhouse.com** to receive a free book.

Or you may write to us at

Harrison House • P.O. Box 35035 • Tulsa, Oklahoma 74153

The Harrison House Vision

Proclaiming the truth and the power

Of the Gospel of Jesus Christ

With excellence;

Challenging Christians to

Live victoriously,

Grow spiritually,

Know God intimately.

Fast. Easy.
Convenient.

For the latest Harrison House product information and author news, look no further than your computer. All the details on our powerful, life-changing products are just a click away. New releases, E-mail subscriptions, testimonies, monthly specials—find it all in one place. Visit harrisonhouse.com today!

harrisonhouse